Central Statistics Office
An Phríomh-Oifig Staidrimh

Demographic, Social and Economic Situation of the Farming Community in 1991

Censuses of Agriculture and Population

Published by the Stationery Office, Dublin, Ireland.

To be purchased from the:

Central Statistics Office, Information Section, Skehard Road, Cork.

Government Publications Sales Office, Sun Alliance House, Molesworth Street, Dublin 2,

or through any bookseller.

Pn 5159   Price £10.00.   April 1998.

Material compiled and presented by
Central Statistics Office.

ISBN 0–7076–1847-9

Table of Contents

General Details

Tables

Appendices

General Details

Introduction

The Census of Population (COP) was taken on the night of Sunday, 21 April 1991. Fieldwork was completed towards the end of May. A Census of Agriculture (COA) was conducted immediately afterwards with 1 June as the reference date. Around 1,300 enumerators were retained from the Census of Population field force to conduct the Census of Agriculture.

A special filter question concerning farming activity was included on the Census of Population questionnaire (see Appendix 2). Replies to this filter question enabled the interviewers to compile a primary list of farmers for interview in the Census of Agriculture.

The combined field operation and the filter question made it possible to link the details relating to a particular family farm with the information contained in the Census of Population return for the corresponding farm household. This publication analyses the main demographic, social and economic characteristics of farm households. Three main sets of analyses are presented:

- the characteristics of the heads of family farm, other rural and urban households are compared;

- family farm operators who gave farming as their principal occupation in the Census of Population are compared with family farm operators who had a different principal occupation;

- the characteristics of members aged 15 and over in the three household types are compared.

Key Concepts

The following definitions should be noted in respect of the key terms used in this Report. A full glossary of terms used is given in Appendix 3.

Head of household: A head of household was identified in the Census of Population for every household. He/she has been used as the focal point for comparisons between family farm, other rural and urban households. Any adult member of a private household, present on Census night, could be returned as the head according as the household members considered appropriate. Non-private households (institutions etc.) have been excluded from the analyses.

Household type: Three household types were identified for the purposes of this publication. *Family farm* households are those households which were recorded as involved in farming on their own account in the Census of Agriculture. A small number of family farm households (2%) were located in urban areas. *Urban* households were located in towns with 1,500 or more inhabitants excluding those that were classified as family farm households. *Other rural* households were comprised of all other households.

Family farm operator: A family farm operator was identified in the Census of Agriculture for each family farm. Family farms accounted for 99.6 per cent of all farms. The owner and the family farm operator was usually the same person. The family farm operator was usually also returned as the head of household in the Census of Population.

Occupation: All persons aged 15 years and over who were at work, unemployed or retired were classified in the Census of Population according to their usual (or previous) principal occupation. Nearly one-third of family farm operators had a principal occupation outside of farming.

Labour force: Only those at work, seeking regular work for the first time or unemployed are in the labour force. Family farm operators who gave their principal economic status as retired are classified as *not in the labour force* in the detailed occupation tables (e.g. Table 15). Hence they are not classified to Agriculture even if their previous occupation was farmer.

COP farmer: This category is derived from the occupation code. Retired farmers are included. Agricultural related jobs such as farm labourers are not included.

Farm type: An EU-wide system known as the *Community Farm Typology* was developed for the purposes of classifying farms into homogeneous groups based on the type of farming activity engaged in. A feature of this classification is the distinction between *specialist* and *mixed* farms. Specialist farms were those where a particular activity such as tillage or dairying accounted for at least two-thirds of the farm's total economic size.

Commentary on Results

Overall importance of farming

A total of 170,578 farms were recorded in the 1991 Census of Agriculture. Of these, 169,893 were classified as family farms. The corresponding family farm households accounted for 16 per cent of all private households in the State. Other rural households accounted for a further 28 per cent and urban households comprised the remaining 56 per cent.

Around 12 per cent of the over-15 population did some farmwork during the twelve months preceding the Census of Agriculture. Leitrim had the highest proportion (37.5%) followed by Roscommon (33.5%), Mayo (32.4%) and Cavan (30.1%). In contrast, only 0.4 per cent of the over-15 population in Dublin were engaged in farmwork.

The total area farmed[1] in 1991 was 4.4 million hectares. This represented almost two-thirds (64.5%) of the area of the State. The average farm size was 26 hectares. A quarter of all family farms were under 10 hectares.

Dairy, beef and mixed grazing were the main farming activities engaged in. There were 6.9 million cattle, 8.9 million sheep, 1.3 million pigs and 12.1 million poultry recorded in the 1991 Census of Agriculture.

Heads of households

The heads of family farm households were more likely to be male, single, older and less formally educated than the heads of other rural or urban households.

Around 88 per cent of the heads of family farm households were male compared to 76 per cent for other rural heads and 69 per cent for urban heads.

---

[1] Areas taken up by commonage, roads, water, bog, unused rough land etc. were excluded.

Around 22 per cent of the heads of family farm households were single. This compared with 16 per cent for other rural heads and 20 per cent for urban heads. Family farms contained the smallest proportion (1%) of separated heads of households.

Table A Heads of households classified by marital status and household type

Household type	Single	Married	Separated [1]	Widowed
Family farm	22%	66%	1%	12%
Other rural	16%	65%	3%	16%
Urban	20%	61%	5%	13%

[1] Including divorced

Around 24 per cent of the heads of family farm households were aged 55-64 compared with 14 per cent for both other rural and urban heads. Around 29 per cent of both family farm and other rural heads were aged 65 and over compared with 20 per cent for urban heads. In contrast, only 8 per cent of family farm heads were aged 15-34 compared with 18 per cent for other rural heads and 26 per cent for urban heads.

Around 63 per cent of farm heads attained primary standard education only compared with 33 per cent for urban heads and 47 per cent for other rural heads.

One-fifth of all households were occupied by only one person. There were more cases of elderly persons living alone in other rural households. Around 58 per cent of persons living alone in other rural households were aged over 65 compared with 41 per cent for both family farm and urban households.

Diagram 1 Heads of household classified by education and household type

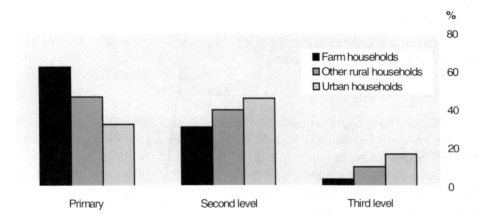

Family farm operators

Family farm operators who were also recorded as farmers in the Census of Population (*COP farmer*) had similarly distinct demographic and social characteristics as those attributed to the heads of farm households. Thus they were more likely to be male, single and less educated than family farm operators who did not have farmer as their principal COP occupation. They also had larger farms and were more involved in intensive farming such as dairying.

Table B presents a summary of the characteristics of both types of family farm operator. Of the 169,893 family farm operators, 72 per cent also recorded themselves as farmers in the Census of Population.

In contrast, only 42 per cent of female family farm operators recorded themselves as COP farmers. Similarly, only 48 per cent of family farm operators farming under 10 hectares were COP farmers.

Around 81 per cent of single family farm operators were COP farmers. Over 89 per cent of specialist dairy farm operators were COP farmers while less than two-thirds (64%) of specialist beef farm operators were COP farmers.

Around 18 per cent of farm operators whose COP principal occupation was not farmer were classified as *Producers, makers and repairers*. A further 9 per cent were included within the broad occupational group *Agriculture* but they were employed as assisting relatives, agricultural labourers, market gardeners, forestry workers etc. rather than as farmers. A further one-third were not in the labour force.

Table B Farm Operators classified by Census of Population principal occupation

Characteristic	COP farmer	Other COP Occupation
All family farm operators	**72%**	**28%**
Female family farm operators	42%	58%
Single family farm operators	81%	19%
Primary education only (or none)	77%	23%
Farm less than 10 hectares	48%	52%
Specialist dairy farmers	89%	11%
Specialist beef farmers	64%	36%

Tables 14-24 examine the characteristics of family farm operators as one group. Around 81 per cent classified themselves as *At work*. A further 3 per cent were *Unemployed*, 10 per cent were *Retired* and 4 per cent were on *Home duties*. Hence 84 per cent of family farm operators were classified as being in the labour force (at work or unemployed).

Around 68 per cent of family farm operators gave *Agriculture* as their principal occupation. The comparable figures for specialist dairying farmers and specialist tillage farmers were 88 per cent and 75 per cent respectively. In contrast, only 57 per cent of specialist beef and 59 per cent of specialist sheep producers gave *Agriculture* as their principal occupation. These percentages would increase significantly if retired farmers were classified to the industry grouping of their former principal occupation rather than to the *Not in the labour force* category.

Over 7,400 farms were operated by Church of Ireland members. Around 48 per cent of these farmed more than 30 hectares compared with 27 per cent of Catholic farmers.

Household members (aged 15 and over)

Table C shows that 52 per cent of persons aged 15 and over in family farm households classified themselves as *At work*. The corresponding figure for other rural households was 40 per cent and 45 per cent for urban households. Only 4 per cent of family farm members were classified as *Unemployed* compared with 10 per cent for both other rural households and urban households.

Half of the persons (aged 15 and over) in other rural households were not part of the labour force. The comparable figure for family farm households was 43 per cent and 45 per cent for urban households.

Table C Principal economic status of persons (aged 15 and over) by household type

| Household type | In labour force | | Not in labour force | | |
	At work	Unemployed	Retired	Home duties	Other[1]
Family farm	52%	4%	7%	23%	13%
Other rural	40%	10%	11%	27%	12%
Urban	45%	10%	8%	22%	14%

[1] Unable to work (sick or disabled) and other.

Table D presents a summary analysis by household type of the occupations of household members aged 15 and over. Family farm operators and other family farm household members are separately distinguished. Agriculture was the main occupation of 12 per cent of the other members of family farm households. Around 4 per cent of the members (aged 15 and over) of other rural households regarded themselves as agricultural employees – see Appendix 2 for treatment of Census of Agriculture family farms that were not matched with a corresponding Census of Population household. Around 13 per cent of the members (aged 15 and over) of other rural households were classified as *Producers, makers and repairers.*

Table D Principal occupations of household members (aged 15 and over) by household type

| Occupation | Family farm households | | Family farm households | Other rural households | Urban households |
	Farm operators	Other farm household members			
Agriculture	68%	12%	32%	4%	1%
Producers	5%	7%	6%	13%	11%
Labourers	2%	2%	2%	4%	3%
Transport	2%	1%	1%	3%	4%
Commerce	2%	4%	3%	6%	7%
Professional	2%	5%	4%	6%	9%
Others	3%	10%	8%	13%	21%
Not in labour force	16%	59%	43%	50%	45%
Total	100%	100%	100%	100%	100%

There were 630,950 persons of all ages recorded in family farm households. The overall ratio of females to males is 84 to 100.

Housing conditions

Three-quarters of family farm households were owner occupied without a mortgage or loan outstanding. Over 35 per cent were built before 1919. Around 47 per cent had central heating while only 23 per cent were connected to the public mains supply - the remainder received their water supply through group schemes and other means.

Tables

Rounding: *A grossing factor was applied to each family farm household to compensate for family farms that were not matched with the respective Census of Population household (see Appendix 2). This resulted in rounding differences between the total for a family farm variable and the sum of its categories in some tables.*

Table 1 Number of family[1] farms classified by farm size[2]

Province and County	Total	Farm size - hectares									
		< 1 [3]	1 - < 2	2 - < 5	5 - < 10	10 - < 20	20 - < 30	30 - < 50	50 - < 100	>= 100
State	169,893	1,446	2,905	14,660	24,088	48,182	30,916	28,339	15,597	3,760
Leinster	42,508	492	979	3,619	4,710	9,113	7,182	8,386	6,245	1,782
Carlow	2,121	39	46	170	186	358	356	463	390	113
Dublin	1,468	61	87	199	193	275	173	201	189	90
Kildare	3,183	36	100	333	366	590	473	507	562	216
Kilkenny	4,417	44	79	258	300	763	735	1,144	912	182
Laoighis	3,918	90	89	310	380	854	689	811	577	118
Longford	3,097	8	36	208	503	1,058	602	479	180	23
Louth	2,268	32	68	348	351	466	316	352	238	97
Meath	5,593	76	142	523	692	1,287	848	970	749	306
Offaly	4,090	14	86	313	472	998	756	827	519	105
Westmeath	4,102	12	79	360	504	1,027	779	752	464	125
Wexford	5,550	45	135	400	506	968	975	1,299	990	232
Wicklow	2,701	35	32	197	257	469	480	581	475	175
Munster	56,245	643	1,054	3,629	5,394	13,350	11,572	12,412	6,740	1,451
Clare	8,207	33	70	436	855	2,429	2,020	1,629	602	133
Cork	17,222	187	265	917	1,444	3,804	3,541	4,213	2,397	454
Kerry	10,849	139	276	963	1,451	2,996	2,126	1,795	847	256
Limerick	7,366	170	181	525	616	1,686	1,576	1,717	790	105
Tipperary NR	4,440	22	72	223	374	948	912	1,094	678	117
Tipperary SR	4,921	59	100	316	390	941	906	1,238	778	193
Waterford	3,240	33	90	249	264	546	491	726	648	193
Connacht	48,920	124	493	4,353	9,575	18,899	8,580	5,043	1,540	313
Galway	16,213	45	224	1,623	2,766	6,090	2,892	1,823	609	141
Leitrim	4,512	7	18	227	899	1,817	863	524	147	10
Mayo	14,881	32	159	1,623	3,449	5,909	2,277	1,068	288	76
Roscommon	7,799	30	45	406	1,333	3,106	1,548	969	318	44
Sligo	5,515	10	47	474	1,128	1,977	1,000	659	178	42
Ulster (part of)	22,220	187	379	3,059	4,409	6,820	3,582	2,498	1,072	214
Cavan	6,701	40	48	578	1,218	2,337	1,356	850	255	19
Donegal	10,214	33	265	1,878	2,079	2,631	1,330	1,149	664	185
Monaghan	5,305	114	66	603	1,112	1,852	896	499	153	10

1 There were an additional 685 non-family farms recorded in the 1991 Census of Agriculture.
2 Source : Census of Agriculture.
3 Only farms less than 1 hectare area farmed engaged in specialised agricultural activity are included - see coverage section in text.

Table 2 Selected 1991 Censuses of Agriculture and Population aggregates

Province and County	Area[1,2]	Area farmed[1,3]	Percentage area farmed	Households[2]	Farms[3]	Percentage farms	Persons over 15[2]	Agriculture workers[3]	Percentage agriculture workers
State	**6,889,456**	**4,441,755**	**64.5%**	**1,032,811**	**170,578**	**16.5%**	**2,585,145**	**312,729**	**12.1%**
Leinster	**1,963,335**	**1,404,698**	**71.6%**	**546,399**	**42,856**	**7.8%**	**1,368,688**	**83,886**	**6.1%**
Carlow	89,635	77,916	86.9%	11,348	2,130	18.8%	29,332	3,922	13.4%
Dublin	92,156	49,212	53.4%	311,958	1,511	0.5%	773,047	3,442	0.4%
Kildare	169,425	122,963	72.6%	33,067	3,251	9.8%	85,749	6,769	7.9%
Kilkenny	206,167	167,801	81.4%	20,714	4,438	21.4%	53,034	8,999	17.0%
Laoighis	171,954	120,887	70.3%	14,441	3,930	27.2%	37,084	7,810	21.1%
Longford	104,387	68,229	65.4%	8,950	3,107	34.7%	21,673	5,139	23.7%
Louth	82,334	63,837	77.5%	25,994	2,280	8.8%	65,475	4,227	6.5%
Meath	233,587	191,654	82.0%	28,868	5,648	19.6%	73,716	10,075	13.7%
Offaly	199,774	120,534	60.3%	16,287	4,107	25.2%	41,609	7,783	18.7%
Westmeath	176,290	118,908	67.4%	17,703	4,127	23.3%	44,739	7,731	17.3%
Wexford	235,143	198,829	84.6%	28,882	5,597	19.4%	73,349	12,650	17.2%
Wicklow	202,483	103,929	51.3%	28,187	2,730	9.7%	69,881	5,339	7.6%
Munster	**2,412,738**	**1,699,858**	**70.4%**	**294,542**	**56,456**	**19.2%**	**740,478**	**108,274**	**14.6%**
Clare	318,784	215,636	67.6%	26,509	8,229	31.0%	65,951	15,007	22.8%
Cork	745,988	549,424	73.6%	119,553	17,298	14.5%	302,614	35,090	11.6%
Kerry	470,142	287,932	61.2%	36,347	10,880	29.9%	90,096	19,125	21.2%
Limerick	268,580	203,157	75.6%	46,726	7,387	15.8%	118,554	13,565	11.4%
Tipperary NR	199,622	144,578	72.4%	16,707	4,450	26.6%	42,087	8,675	20.6%
Tipperary SR	225,836	170,420	75.5%	21,889	4,956	22.6%	54,233	9,950	18.4%
Waterford	183,786	128,711	70.0%	26,811	3,256	12.1%	66,943	6,862	10.2%
Connacht	**1,712,172**	**909,509**	**53.1%**	**124,640**	**49,004**	**39.3%**	**309,801**	**83,441**	**26.9%**
Galway	593,966	320,471	54.0%	51,025	16,244	31.8%	132,213	28,731	21.7%
Leitrim	152,476	84,975	55.7%	8,273	4,516	54.6%	18,768	7,045	37.5%
Mayo	539,846	242,174	44.9%	32,919	14,909	45.3%	80,270	25,982	32.4%
Roscommon	246,276	156,134	63.4%	15,921	7,811	49.1%	38,089	12,775	33.5%
Sligo	179,608	105,755	58.9%	16,502	5,524	33.5%	40,461	8,908	22.0%
Ulster (part of)	**801,211**	**427,690**	**53.4%**	**67,230**	**22,262**	**33.1%**	**166,178**	**37,128**	**22.3%**
Cavan	189,060	129,068	68.3%	15,779	6,719	42.6%	38,084	11,463	30.1%
Donegal	483,058	210,096	43.5%	36,744	10,228	27.8%	91,542	16,412	17.9%
Monaghan	129,093	88,525	68.6%	14,707	5,315	36.1%	36,552	9,253	25.3%

1 In hectares.
2 Source : Census of Population.
3 Source : Census of Agriculture.

Table 3 Heads of household[1] classified by marital status[2] and household type[3]

Household type	All households[4]	Marital status				
		Single	Married	Separated[5]	Widowed
All households	**1,060,644**	**204,750**	**668,634**	**42,606**	**144,655**
Family farm households	169,893	36,630	112,462	1,247	19,555
Other rural households	298,002	47,237	192,742	8,878	49,145
Urban households	592,749	120,883	363,430	32,481	75,955

1 The head of a family farm household is not necessarily the farmer.
2 Source : Census of Population.
3 Source : Census of Population and Census of Agriculture.
4 See Appendix 2 note on correct number of households.
5 Including divorced.

Table 4 Heads of household[1] classified by age[2] and household type[3]

Household type	All households[4]	Age					
		15 - 34	35 - 44	45 - 54	55 - 64	65+
All households	**1,060,644**	**219,643**	**230,714**	**187,465**	**166,490**	**256,332**
Family farm households	169,893	13,884	30,839	35,190	40,160	49,820
Other rural households	298,002	53,330	68,881	48,469	40,444	86,878
Urban households	592,749	152,429	130,994	103,806	85,886	119,634

1 The head of a family farm household is not necessarily the farmer.
2 Source : Census of Population.
3 Source : Census of Population and Census of Agriculture.
4 See Appendix 2 note on correct number of households.

Table 5 Heads of household[1] classified by education[2] and household type[3]

| Household type | All households[4] | Highest level of education completed | | | | |
| | | Primary (incl. no formal education) | Second level | | Third level | Not stated |
			First stage	Second stage		
All households	**1,060,644**	**440,834**	**187,504**	**261,854**	**140,443**	**30,010**
Family farm households	169,893	106,371	26,452	26,661	7,526	2,884
Other rural households	298,002	140,127	53,946	66,686	31,576	5,667
Urban households	592,749	194,336	107,106	168,507	101,341	21,459

1 The head of a family farm household is not necessarily the farmer.
2 Source : Census of Population.
3 Source : Census of Population and Census of Agriculture.
4 See Appendix 2 note on correct number of households.

Table 6 Household members classified by sex[1] and household type[2]

| Household type | All household members[3] | Heads of household | | Other household members | |
		Males	Females	Males	Females
All households	**3,546,059**	**786,189**	**274,455**	**984,819**	**1,500,596**
Family farm households	630,950	149,859	20,034	192,819	268,238
Other rural households	983,806	225,291	72,711	268,151	417,653
Urban households	1,931,303	411,039	181,710	523,849	814,705

1 Source : Census of Population.
2 Source : Census of Population and Census of Agriculture.
3 See Appendix 2 note on correct number of households.

Table 7 Households¹ classified by household composition² and age of head of household²

Household type and age of head	All households³	Household composition				
		One person	Husband and wife (or couple)	Husband and wife (or couple) with children and/or other persons	Lone parent with one or more children with/without other persons	Other
All households	**1,060,644**	**213,058**	**128,871**	**525,027**	**112,835**	**80,854**
Age						
15 - 34	219,643	31,001	32,501	109,669	18,806	27,665
35 - 44	230,714	22,207	10,835	168,985	21,553	7,134
45 - 54	187,465	24,493	11,082	124,258	20,060	7,572
55 - 64	166,490	36,390	23,340	73,760	20,662	12,338
65+	256,332	98,967	51,113	48,354	31,754	26,144
Family farm households	**169,893**	**26,129**	**16,761**	**93,894**	**18,139**	**14,971**
Age						
15 - 34	13,884	1,074	2,009	8,903	1,067	830
35 - 44	30,839	2,309	1,288	23,699	2,190	1,353
45 - 54	35,190	4,454	1,629	24,126	3,014	1,967
55 - 64	40,160	7,472	4,017	20,303	4,448	3,920
65+	49,820	10,820	7,818	16,862	7,420	6,900
Other rural households	**298,002**	**65,931**	**40,166**	**146,437**	**28,055**	**17,413**
Age						
15 - 34	53,330	4,651	8,822	34,254	3,168	2,435
35 - 44	68,881	5,018	3,494	53,795	5,177	1,397
45 - 54	48,469	6,617	3,550	31,491	4,912	1,899
55 - 64	40,444	11,098	6,418	14,687	5,104	3,137
65+	86,878	38,547	17,882	12,210	9,694	8,545
Urban households	**592,749**	**120,998**	**71,944**	**284,696**	**66,641**	**48,470**
Age						
15 - 34	152,429	25,276	21,670	66,512	14,571	24,400
35 - 44	130,994	14,880	6,053	91,491	14,186	4,384
45 - 54	103,806	13,422	5,903	68,641	12,134	3,706
55 - 64	85,886	17,820	12,905	38,770	11,110	5,281
65+	119,634	49,600	25,413	19,282	14,640	10,699

1 The head of a family farm household is not necessarily the farmer.
2 Source : Census of Population.
3 See Appendix 2 note on correct number of households.

Table 8 Family farm operators classified by marital status[1] and occupation[1]

Family farm operators	Marital status				
	Total	Single	Married	Separated[2]	Widowed
Family farm operators	**169,893**	**45,930**	**109,024**	**1,250**	**13,689**
COP[3] farmer[4]	122,544	37,385	76,257	723	8,180
Other COP occupation	47,349	8,546	32,767	527	5,509

1 Source : Census of Population.
2 Including divorced.
3 COP = Census of Population.
4 COP farmer is a farm operator who recorded their current (or former) principal occupation as "farmer" in the Census of Population.

Table 9 Family farm operators classified by age,[1] occupation[1] and sex[1]

Family farm operators	Age					
	Total	15 - 34	35 - 44	45 - 54	55 - 64	65+
Family farm operators	**169,893**	**19,980**	**33,787**	**36,027**	**38,820**	**41,278**
COP farmer[2]	122,544	12,818	21,881	25,492	30,156	32,199
Male	115,681	12,528	21,301	24,325	27,956	29,572
Female	6,863	290	579	1,167	2,200	2,627
Other COP occupation	47,349	7,162	11,906	10,536	8,665	9,080
Male	37,759	6,165	10,479	9,056	6,655	5,404
Female	9,590	997	1,428	1,480	2,010	3,675

1 Source : Census of Population.
2 COP farmer is a farm operator who recorded their current (or former) principal occupation as "farmer" in the Census of Population.

Table 10 Family farm operators classified by education[1] and occupation[1]

Family farm operators	Highest level of education completed					
	Total	Primary (incl. no formal education)	Second level		Third level	Not stated
			First stage	Second stage		
Family farm operators	**169,893**	**101,547**	**29,154**	**28,780**	**7,448**	**2,964**
COP farmer[2]	122,544	78,324	20,742	18,581	2,812	2,084
Other COP occupation	47,349	23,223	8,412	10,199	4,636	880

1 Source : Census of Population.
2 COP farmer is a farm operator who recorded their current (or former) principal occupation as "farmer" in the Census of Population.

Table 11 Family farm operators classified by farm size[1] and occupation[2]

Family farm operators	Farm size - hectares								
	Total	< 1	1 - < 5	5 - < 10	10 - < 20	20 - < 30	30 - < 50	50 - < 100	>= 100
Family farm operators	**169,893**	**1,446**	**17,565**	**24,088**	**48,182**	**30,916**	**28,339**	**15,597**	**3,760**
COP farmer[3]	122,544	381	6,701	13,591	34,028	25,360	24,902	14,200	3,381
Other COP occupation	47,349	1,065	10,864	10,497	14,154	5,556	3,437	1,397	379

1 Source : Census of Agriculture.
2 Source : Census of Population.
3 COP farmer is a farm operator who recorded their current (or former) principal occupation as "farmer" in the Census of Population.

Table 12 Family farm operators classified by farm type[1] and occupation[2]

Family farm operators	Total	Farm type						
		Specialist tillage	Specialist dairying	Specialist beef production	Specialist sheep	Mixed grazing livestock	Mixed crops and livestock	Other
Family farm operators	**169,893**	**4,787**	**44,906**	**69,504**	**14,406**	**29,579**	**4,240**	**2,472**
COP farmer[3]	122,544	3,470	40,169	44,270	9,323	20,514	3,549	1,249
Other COP occupation	47,349	1,317	4,737	25,234	5,083	9,064	690	1,223

1 Source : Census of Agriculture.
2 Source : Census of Population.
3 COP farmer is a farm operator who recorded their current (or former) principal occupation as "farmer" in the Census of Population.

Table 13 Family farm operators classified by occupation[1]

Family farm operators	Total	In labour force							Not in labour force
		Agriculture, forestry and fishermen[2]	Producers, makers and repairers	Labourers and unskilled workers (n.e.s.)	Transport and communication workers	Commerce, insurance and finance workers	Professional and technical workers	Others	
Family farm operators	**169,893**	**115,724**	**8,739**	**4,096**	**3,268**	**3,609**	**3,117**	**4,350**	**26,990**
COP farmer[3]	122,544	111,378	–	–	–	–	–	–	11,166
Other COP occupation	47,349	4,346	8,739	4,096	3,268	3,609	3,117	4,350	15,824

1 Source : Census of Population.
2 The 4,346 *Agricultural* workers include assisting relatives, agricultural labourers, market gardeners, forestry workers etc.
3 COP farmer is a farm operator who recorded their current (or former) principal occupation as "farmer" in the Census of Population.

Table 14 Family farm operators classified by principal economic status[1]

Province and County	Total	At work	Unemployed[2]	Retired	Home duties	Unable to work (sick or disabled)	Other
State	**169,893**	**138,354**	**4,549**	**16,838**	**7,287**	**2,727**	**138**
Leinster	**42,508**	**36,080**	**817**	**3,307**	**1,717**	**535**	**51**
Carlow	2,121	1,846	46	130	65	32	2
Dublin	1,468	1,267	14	93	77	14	2
Kildare	3,183	2,685	49	297	115	33	5
Kilkenny	4,417	4,036	44	218	91	27	1
Laoighis	3,918	3,421	80	282	99	35	–
Longford	3,097	2,498	52	277	214	52	4
Louth	2,268	1,740	86	269	130	36	7
Meath	5,593	4,590	141	464	300	88	10
Offaly	4,090	3,420	97	371	136	64	2
Westmeath	4,102	3,347	83	417	186	64	5
Wexford	5,550	4,949	81	283	182	52	4
Wicklow	2,701	2,281	45	206	121	38	9
Munster	**56,245**	**48,509**	**943**	**4,137**	**1,986**	**625**	**45**
Clare	8,207	7,030	107	687	283	94	7
Cork	17,222	15,181	228	1,077	593	128	16
Kerry	10,849	8,840	310	1,087	437	169	5
Limerick	7,366	6,353	143	529	235	103	4
Tipperary NR	4,440	3,993	55	206	139	45	1
Tipperary SR	4,921	4,282	57	326	190	58	8
Waterford	3,240	2,831	44	224	109	29	4
Connacht	**48,920**	**37,737**	**1,554**	**6,163**	**2,404**	**1,042**	**21**
Galway	16,213	12,365	652	2,012	844	334	6
Leitrim	4,512	3,309	149	664	232	154	5
Mayo	14,881	11,366	413	1,973	821	303	5
Roscommon	7,799	6,424	144	802	301	127	1
Sligo	5,515	4,273	196	713	206	124	4
Ulster (part of)	**22,220**	**16,028**	**1,234**	**3,231**	**1,181**	**525**	**21**
Cavan	6,701	5,684	162	532	246	74	5
Donegal	10,214	6,023	958	2,106	734	377	16
Monaghan	5,305	4,321	114	594	202	74	1

Principal economic status

1 Source : Census of Population.
2 Includes persons looking for first regular job.

Table 15 Family farm operators classified by occupation[1]

Province and County	Total	In labour force							Not in labour force
		Agriculture, forestry and fishermen	Producers, makers and repairers	Labourers and unskilled workers (n.e.s.)	Transport and communication workers	Commerce, insurance and finance workers	Professional and technical workers	Others	
State	**169,893**	**115,724**	**8,739**	**4,096**	**3,268**	**3,609**	**3,117**	**4,350**	**26,990**
Leinster	**42,508**	**29,878**	**2,268**	**683**	**778**	**1,047**	**948**	**1,295**	**5,610**
Carlow	2,121	1,615	65	45	41	39	40	48	229
Dublin	1,468	908	76	7	27	67	101	95	186
Kildare	3,183	2,085	176	46	66	112	95	154	449
Kilkenny	4,417	3,542	159	34	82	88	78	96	338
Laoighis	3,918	2,951	187	61	84	65	71	81	417
Longford	3,097	1,983	235	62	60	62	56	91	547
Louth	2,268	1,322	158	33	74	78	59	103	442
Meath	5,593	3,649	349	126	85	165	148	208	862
Offaly	4,090	2,786	324	99	74	81	48	105	573
Westmeath	4,102	2,644	280	77	63	111	106	150	672
Wexford	5,550	4,450	157	62	77	101	87	96	520
Wicklow	2,701	1,943	102	31	45	77	59	68	375
Munster	**56,245**	**42,101**	**2,084**	**1,047**	**892**	**1,069**	**1,010**	**1,250**	**6,792**
Clare	8,207	5,826	414	180	182	160	149	225	1,070
Cork	17,222	13,486	550	256	241	277	270	328	1,814
Kerry	10,849	7,738	441	253	158	198	154	206	1,699
Limerick	7,366	5,347	310	164	123	180	172	200	871
Tipperary NR	4,440	3,484	117	64	80	104	83	116	391
Tipperary SR	4,921	3,758	145	69	57	89	109	112	582
Waterford	3,240	2,463	105	61	50	60	72	64	366
Connacht	**48,920**	**30,570**	**2,973**	**1,546**	**1,042**	**1,005**	**881**	**1,274**	**9,629**
Galway	16,213	10,445	748	523	327	296	267	410	3,196
Leitrim	4,512	2,369	450	180	118	112	98	130	1,054
Mayo	14,881	9,324	868	491	290	251	231	324	3,102
Roscommon	7,799	5,070	554	199	182	189	159	216	1,231
Sligo	5,515	3,361	353	154	124	157	125	194	1,046
Ulster (part of)	**22,220**	**13,174**	**1,415**	**819**	**556**	**488**	**279**	**531**	**4,958**
Cavan	6,701	4,607	440	197	186	156	97	162	855
Donegal	10,214	5,032	594	501	228	231	119	276	3,232
Monaghan	5,305	3,536	381	121	141	101	64	92	870

1 Source : Census of Population.

Table 16 Family farm operators classified by marital status[1]

Province and County		Marital status				
	Total	Single	Married	Separated[2]	Widowed
State	**169,893**	**45,930**	**109,024**	**1,250**	**13,689**
Leinster	**42,508**	**10,132**	**28,864**	**384**	**3,128**
Carlow	2,121	547	1,410	11	154
Dublin	1,468	246	1,096	26	101
Kildare	3,183	617	2,271	36	259
Kilkenny	4,417	1,156	2,968	32	261
Laoighis	3,918	1,016	2,584	25	293
Longford	3,097	879	1,908	12	297
Louth	2,268	533	1,532	23	179
Meath	5,593	1,089	4,006	56	442
Offaly	4,090	1,104	2,682	33	271
Westmeath	4,102	1,104	2,660	32	305
Wexford	5,550	1,171	3,917	60	401
Wicklow	2,701	670	1,829	37	164
Munster	**56,245**	**15,323**	**36,514**	**372**	**4,036**
Clare	8,207	2,446	5,111	56	594
Cork	17,222	4,622	11,348	117	1,135
Kerry	10,849	3,218	6,691	71	869
Limerick	7,366	1,812	4,962	61	531
Tipperary NR	4,440	1,213	2,924	17	285
Tipperary SR	4,921	1,151	3,329	30	410
Waterford	3,240	861	2,148	19	212
Connacht	**48,920**	**13,816**	**30,021**	**334**	**4,748**
Galway	16,213	4,300	10,157	94	1,662
Leitrim	4,512	1,441	2,614	38	420
Mayo	14,881	4,180	9,073	104	1,523
Roscommon	7,799	2,232	4,815	51	700
Sligo	5,515	1,662	3,363	47	443
Ulster (part of)	**22,220**	**6,658**	**13,625**	**160**	**1,777**
Cavan	6,701	2,253	3,977	28	443
Donegal	10,214	2,919	6,242	96	956
Monaghan	5,305	1,486	3,406	35	378

1 Source : Census of Population.
2 Including divorced.

Table 17   Family farm operators classified by education[1]

Province and County	Total	Primary (incl. no formal education)	Highest level of education completed				Not stated
			Second level				
			First stage	Second stage	Third level		
State	**169,893**	**101,547**	**29,154**	**28,780**	**7,448**		**2,964**
Leinster	**42,508**	**22,370**	**8,514**	**8,273**	**2,671**		**680**
Carlow	2,121	1,153	464	345	119		40
Dublin	1,468	586	255	371	224		31
Kildare	3,183	1,326	730	732	326		69
Kilkenny	4,417	2,134	1,117	870	244		52
Laoighis	3,918	2,342	785	612	155		24
Longford	3,097	1,829	481	620	114		54
Louth	2,268	1,160	451	460	158		38
Meath	5,593	2,619	1,095	1,303	441		135
Offaly	4,090	2,443	737	714	150		47
Westmeath	4,102	2,190	761	844	242		64
Wexford	5,550	3,104	1,167	902	302		74
Wicklow	2,701	1,483	471	501	194		52
Munster	**56,245**	**30,342**	**11,500**	**10,644**	**2,767**		**991**
Clare	8,207	4,796	1,453	1,466	329		164
Cork	17,222	9,309	3,695	3,103	873		242
Kerry	10,849	6,751	1,794	1,697	341		266
Limerick	7,366	3,494	1,646	1,652	443		131
Tipperary NR	4,440	2,287	1,000	889	222		42
Tipperary SR	4,921	2,148	1,172	1,164	342		95
Waterford	3,240	1,559	739	674	217		51
Connacht	**48,920**	**33,111**	**6,447**	**7,126**	**1,413**		**822**
Galway	16,213	11,384	1,986	2,089	434		319
Leitrim	4,512	2,762	756	768	134		92
Mayo	14,881	10,695	1,684	1,922	364		216
Roscommon	7,799	4,976	1,180	1,298	245		101
Sligo	5,515	3,294	841	1,048	237		95
Ulster (part of)	**22,220**	**15,723**	**2,693**	**2,736**	**597**		**471**
Cavan	6,701	4,518	953	882	201		147
Donegal	10,214	7,760	872	1,112	252		218
Monaghan	5,305	3,444	868	742	144		106

1 Source : Census of Population.

Table 18 Family farm operators classified by age[1]

Province and County	Total	Age				
		15 - 34	35 - 44	45 - 54	55 - 64	65+
State	**169,893**	**19,980**	**33,787**	**36,027**	**38,820**	**41,278**
Leinster	**42,508**	**5,383**	**8,760**	**9,287**	**9,732**	**9,346**
Carlow	2,121	245	450	473	512	441
Dublin	1,468	181	312	349	344	281
Kildare	3,183	382	684	720	694	702
Kilkenny	4,417	659	936	973	983	867
Laoighis	3,918	541	777	848	914	838
Longford	3,097	374	614	614	713	783
Louth	2,268	228	474	460	518	587
Meath	5,593	627	1,197	1,208	1,297	1,264
Offaly	4,090	541	804	869	969	908
Westmeath	4,102	508	775	863	962	994
Wexford	5,550	723	1,171	1,305	1,268	1,083
Wicklow	2,701	375	566	605	558	598
Munster	**56,245**	**7,445**	**11,963**	**12,295**	**12,932**	**11,610**
Clare	8,207	1,089	1,657	1,748	1,855	1,858
Cork	17,222	2,540	3,737	3,764	3,962	3,219
Kerry	10,849	1,264	2,303	2,410	2,507	2,366
Limerick	7,366	901	1,634	1,639	1,721	1,471
Tipperary NR	4,440	606	991	944	1,019	879
Tipperary SR	4,921	620	975	1,047	1,150	1,129
Waterford	3,240	425	667	742	718	689
Connacht	**48,920**	**4,572**	**8,878**	**9,961**	**11,140**	**14,368**
Galway	16,213	1,419	2,868	3,446	3,686	4,793
Leitrim	4,512	469	852	941	985	1,266
Mayo	14,881	1,283	2,703	2,956	3,330	4,609
Roscommon	7,799	760	1,396	1,535	1,872	2,236
Sligo	5,515	641	1,060	1,084	1,267	1,464
Ulster (part of)	**22,220**	**2,580**	**4,185**	**4,484**	**5,017**	**5,954**
Cavan	6,701	954	1,334	1,320	1,602	1,491
Donegal	10,214	915	1,739	2,094	2,224	3,241
Monaghan	5,305	711	1,112	1,070	1,191	1,222

1 Source : Census of Population.

Table 19 Family farm operators classified by occupation[1] and farm size[2]

Farm size - hectares	Total	In labour force							Not in labour force
		Agriculture, forestry and fishermen	Producers, makers and repairers	Labourers and unskilled workers (n.e.s.)	Transport and communication workers	Commerce, insurance and finance workers	Professional and technical workers	Others	
Family farm operators	**169,893**	**115,724**	**8,739**	**4,096**	**3,268**	**3,609**	**3,117**	**4,350**	**26,990**
Farm size - hectares									
< 1	1,446	643	112	45	53	52	91	69	380
1 - < 5	17,565	5,363	1,812	1,103	681	693	667	921	6,326
5 - < 10	24,088	11,347	2,079	1,047	779	751	597	893	6,595
10 - < 20	48,182	31,403	3,012	1,276	1,128	1,079	823	1,338	8,123
20 - < 30	30,916	24,655	1,066	380	372	517	420	598	2,909
30 - < 50	28,339	24,707	501	167	191	347	331	343	1,753
50 - < 100	15,597	14,218	132	60	54	133	157	138	705
>= 100	3,760	3,389	27	17	10	36	32	50	199

1 Source : Census of Population.
2 Source : Census of Agriculture.

Table 20 Family farm operators classified by occupation[1] and farm type[2]

Farm type	Total	In labour force							Not in labour force
		Agriculture, forestry and fishermen	Producers, makers and repairers	Labourers and unskilled workers (n.e.s.)	Transport and communication workers	Commerce, insurance and finance workers	Professional and technical workers	Others	
Family farm operators	**169,893**	**115,724**	**8,739**	**4,096**	**3,268**	**3,609**	**3,117**	**4,350**	**26,990**
Farm type									
Specialist tillage	4,787	3,593	146	50	79	145	146	164	464
Specialist dairying	44,906	39,635	775	365	297	211	207	332	3,083
Specialist beef production	69,504	39,462	5,232	2,392	1,927	1,985	1,459	2,153	14,894
Specialist sheep	14,406	8,552	918	570	317	405	394	476	2,776
Mixed grazing livestock	29,579	19,194	1,460	665	564	727	735	1,065	5,168
Mixed crops and livestock	4,240	3,495	102	28	46	69	64	91	346
Other	2,472	1,792	106	26	37	66	114	70	261

1 Source : Census of Population.
2 Source : Census of Agriculture.

Table 21 Family farm operators classified by marital status[1] and farm type[2]

Farm type	Marital status				
	Total	Single	Married	Separated[3]	Widowed
Family farm operators	**169,893**	**45,930**	**109,024**	**1,250**	**13,689**
Farm type					
Specialist tillage	4,787	888	3,611	55	233
Specialist dairying	44,906	10,040	32,197	160	2,509
Specialist beef production	69,504	22,078	40,004	537	6,884
Specialist sheep	14,406	3,897	9,219	134	1,156
Mixed grazing livestock	29,579	7,814	18,929	302	2,534
Mixed crops and livestock	4,240	867	3,087	30	255
Other	2,472	347	1,976	32	118

1 Source : Census of Population.
2 Source : Census of Agriculture.
3 Including divorced.

Table 22 Family farm operators classified by education[1] and farm size[2]

Farm size - hectares	Highest level of education completed					
	Total	Primary (incl. no formal education)	Second level		Third level	Not stated
			First stage	Second stage		
Family farm operators	**169,893**	**101,547**	**29,154**	**28,780**	**7,448**	**2,964**
Farm size - hectares						
< 1	1,446	611	219	368	230	17
1 - < 5	17,565	11,161	2,136	2,676	1,260	332
5 - < 10	24,088	16,317	2,947	3,380	985	459
10 - < 20	48,182	31,484	7,010	7,230	1,527	931
20 - < 30	30,916	18,268	5,592	5,446	1,086	524
30 - < 50	28,339	15,101	6,262	5,432	1,117	428
50 - < 100	15,597	7,129	4,001	3,353	905	210
>= 100	3,760	1,476	987	896	338	62

1 Source : Census of Population.
2 Source : Census of Agriculture.

Table 23 Family farm operators classified by education[1] and farm type[2]

Farm type		Highest level of education completed				
	Total	Primary (incl. no formal education)	Second level		Third level	Not stated
			First stage	Second stage		
Family farm operators	**169,893**	**101,547**	**29,154**	**28,780**	**7,448**	**2,964**
Farm type						
Specialist tillage	4,787	1,899	1,224	1,094	517	53
Specialist dairying	44,906	25,375	9,597	8,049	1,108	777
Specialist beef production	69,504	44,972	9,975	10,838	2,486	1,233
Specialist sheep	14,406	8,969	2,055	2,272	843	266
Mixed grazing livestock	29,579	17,543	4,738	5,013	1,727	557
Mixed crops and livestock	4,240	1,963	1,051	890	277	59
Other	2,472	824	513	625	490	20

1 Source : Census of Population.
2 Source : Census of Agriculture.

Table 24 Family farm operators classified by farm size[1] and religion[2]

Religion		Farm size - hectares							
	Total	< 1	1 - < 5	5 - < 10	10 - < 20	20 - < 30	30 - < 50	50 - < 100	>= 100
Family farm operators	**169,893**	**1,446**	**17,565**	**24,088**	**48,182**	**30,916**	**28,339**	**15,597**	**3,760**
Religion									
Catholic	155,521	1,264	16,165	22,496	45,101	28,452	25,523	13,462	3,058
Church of Ireland	7,432	65	536	669	1,346	1,267	1,621	1,434	494
Other stated religions	2,744	37	232	284	608	504	557	398	124
No religion and not stated	4,197	80	632	638	1,127	692	639	303	84

1 Source : Census of Agriculture.
2 Source : Census of Population.

Table 25 Persons (aged 15 and over) in family farm households classified by principal economic status[1]

Province and County	Principal economic status						
	Total	At work	Unemployed[2]	Retired	Home duties	Unable to work (sick or disabled)	Other
State	**474,342**	**248,013**	**21,205**	**34,383**	**110,345**	**9,235**	**51,161**
Leinster	**121,848**	**66,487**	**4,245**	**6,983**	**28,507**	**1,915**	**13,711**
Carlow	6,155	3,344	213	325	1,464	118	691
Dublin	4,600	2,645	140	195	962	46	611
Kildare	9,127	5,009	320	532	2,063	131	1,072
Kilkenny	12,969	7,455	292	735	2,907	152	1,428
Laoighis	11,187	6,011	434	619	2,695	197	1,232
Longford	8,186	4,350	266	521	2,035	122	893
Louth	6,707	3,448	371	437	1,580	107	765
Meath	16,157	8,584	655	885	3,849	245	1,938
Offaly	11,633	6,269	442	741	2,677	221	1,284
Westmeath	11,131	5,999	401	760	2,542	188	1,241
Wexford	16,332	9,229	441	759	3,905	261	1,737
Wicklow	7,664	4,142	271	474	1,829	129	819
Munster	**159,523**	**86,901**	**5,482**	**10,939**	**35,861**	**2,550**	**17,790**
Clare	22,034	11,640	759	1,719	5,098	377	2,441
Cork	50,298	27,913	1,491	3,342	11,206	662	5,683
Kerry	30,432	15,492	1,523	2,444	7,141	601	3,232
Limerick	20,881	11,760	701	1,356	4,271	343	2,449
Tipperary NR	12,775	7,155	336	675	2,983	210	1,417
Tipperary SR	13,965	7,837	408	857	3,083	220	1,561
Waterford	9,139	5,103	264	546	2,081	137	1,008
Connacht	**132,011**	**65,082**	**7,133**	**11,043**	**31,372**	**3,256**	**14,126**
Galway	45,794	22,607	2,812	3,722	10,560	1,072	5,021
Leitrim	11,179	5,516	570	1,033	2,684	321	1,056
Mayo	40,076	18,894	2,252	3,561	9,928	1,078	4,362
Roscommon	20,629	10,834	743	1,461	4,922	433	2,237
Sligo	14,332	7,231	755	1,266	3,278	351	1,451
Ulster (part of)	**60,960**	**29,544**	**4,346**	**5,418**	**14,604**	**1,514**	**5,534**
Cavan	17,906	9,660	694	1,197	4,399	308	1,647
Donegal	28,324	12,057	2,967	3,168	6,741	909	2,482
Monaghan	14,731	7,826	686	1,052	3,465	297	1,405

1 Source : Census of Population.
2 Includes persons looking for first regular job.

Table 26 Persons (aged 15 and over) in family farm households classified by occupation[1]

Province and County	Total	In labour force							Not in labour force
		Agriculture, forestry and fishermen	Producers, makers and repairers	Labourers and unskilled workers (n.e.s.)	Transport and communication workers	Commerce, insurance and finance workers	Professional and technical workers	Others	
State	**474,342**	**151,396**	**30,439**	**10,988**	**6,993**	**14,814**	**18,554**	**36,034**	**205,124**
Leinster	**121,848**	**40,652**	**7,344**	**1,863**	**1,752**	**4,029**	**5,340**	**9,751**	**51,117**
Carlow	6,155	2,167	334	97	72	182	281	424	2,599
Dublin	4,600	1,312	227	31	88	221	315	592	1,814
Kildare	9,127	2,876	516	117	142	337	479	862	3,799
Kilkenny	12,969	4,915	636	125	178	362	611	922	5,222
Laoighis	11,187	3,969	615	159	159	296	473	774	4,742
Longford	8,186	2,591	594	164	117	246	312	592	3,570
Louth	6,707	1,825	500	123	151	255	306	659	2,889
Meath	16,157	4,955	1,023	311	210	593	686	1,461	6,918
Offaly	11,633	3,666	1,004	224	179	418	412	808	4,922
Westmeath	11,131	3,361	847	200	153	390	541	908	4,731
Wexford	16,332	6,251	705	212	203	466	646	1,188	6,661
Wicklow	7,664	2,765	346	101	100	263	279	560	3,251
Munster	**159,523**	**56,947**	**8,110**	**3,029**	**1,925**	**4,568**	**6,595**	**11,208**	**67,141**
Clare	22,034	7,125	1,261	526	353	634	868	1,631	9,635
Cork	50,298	18,995	2,385	846	522	1,332	1,991	3,334	20,893
Kerry	30,432	10,096	1,817	745	319	906	1,009	2,123	13,417
Limerick	20,881	7,303	1,174	340	292	672	1,086	1,594	8,420
Tipperary NR	12,775	4,616	576	161	197	407	592	941	5,284
Tipperary SR	13,965	5,376	548	183	123	402	632	981	5,720
Waterford	9,139	3,436	349	228	119	216	415	604	3,771
Connacht	**132,011**	**37,027**	**9,602**	**4,129**	**2,144**	**4,369**	**4,784**	**10,160**	**59,796**
Galway	45,794	13,091	3,027	1,708	737	1,603	1,600	3,652	20,375
Leitrim	11,179	2,809	1,079	396	202	331	411	858	5,093
Mayo	40,076	11,104	2,840	1,240	606	1,235	1,342	2,781	18,930
Roscommon	20,629	6,066	1,585	439	357	699	833	1,599	9,053
Sligo	14,332	3,957	1,071	347	242	501	598	1,270	6,345
Ulster (part of)	**60,960**	**16,770**	**5,383**	**1,966**	**1,172**	**1,847**	**1,836**	**4,915**	**27,070**
Cavan	17,906	5,691	1,311	441	370	531	589	1,420	7,552
Donegal	28,324	6,586	2,639	1,212	486	892	752	2,457	13,300
Monaghan	14,731	4,493	1,433	313	316	425	495	1,037	6,219

1 Source : Census of Population.

Table 27 Persons (aged 15 and over) in family farm households classified by marital status[1]

Province and County	Total	Marital status			
		Single	Married	Separated[2]	Widowed
State	**474,342**	**204,123**	**235,022**	**2,053**	**33,143**
Leinster	**121,848**	**52,200**	**61,519**	**641**	**7,488**
Carlow	6,155	2,736	3,006	23	390
Dublin	4,600	2,110	2,272	38	180
Kildare	9,127	3,786	4,748	59	535
Kilkenny	12,969	5,654	6,422	47	846
Laoighis	11,187	4,809	5,561	42	774
Longford	8,186	3,405	4,117	31	633
Louth	6,707	3,068	3,228	40	372
Meath	16,157	6,811	8,364	99	883
Offaly	11,633	5,081	5,779	50	723
Westmeath	11,131	4,737	5,656	48	690
Wexford	16,332	6,778	8,421	101	1,032
Wicklow	7,664	3,225	3,946	63	431
Munster	**159,523**	**68,903**	**79,178**	**619**	**10,823**
Clare	22,034	9,196	11,177	93	1,569
Cork	50,298	22,066	24,722	181	3,329
Kerry	30,432	13,404	14,659	112	2,256
Limerick	20,881	8,907	10,544	94	1,336
Tipperary NR	12,775	5,539	6,354	36	845
Tipperary SR	13,965	5,828	7,120	58	959
Waterford	9,139	3,962	4,601	45	530
Connacht	**132,011**	**55,798**	**65,018**	**534**	**10,661**
Galway	45,794	19,953	22,087	163	3,591
Leitrim	11,179	4,621	5,612	54	891
Mayo	40,076	16,697	19,719	175	3,485
Roscommon	20,629	8,623	10,363	75	1,568
Sligo	14,332	5,903	7,236	67	1,125
Ulster (part of)	**60,960**	**27,223**	**29,307**	**259**	**4,170**
Cavan	17,906	7,829	8,706	43	1,327
Donegal	28,324	12,888	13,334	165	1,937
Monaghan	14,731	6,507	7,267	51	906

1 Source : Census of Population.
2 Including divorced.

CSO Census of Agriculture/Census of Population 1991

Table 28 Persons (aged 15 and over) in other rural households[1] classified by principal economic status[2]

Province and County	Principal economic status						
	Total	At work	Unemployed[3]	Retired	Home duties	Unable to work (sick or disabled)	Other
State	**687,245**	**275,636**	**68,682**	**73,053**	**184,126**	**21,484**	**64,264**
Leinster	**257,615**	**106,377**	**25,934**	**23,006**	**69,465**	**7,454**	**25,379**
Carlow	10,798	4,181	1,285	931	3,005	344	1,052
Dublin	16,290	7,673	1,360	1,173	3,873	298	1,913
Kildare	29,164	12,448	3,027	2,029	7,717	841	3,102
Kilkenny	26,539	10,898	2,760	2,584	7,128	731	2,438
Laoighis	17,130	6,822	1,709	1,659	4,881	517	1,542
Longford	10,026	3,661	959	1,116	3,039	356	895
Louth	18,793	7,863	2,007	1,652	4,764	487	2,020
Meath	38,320	16,719	3,393	3,043	10,125	964	4,076
Offaly	17,206	6,868	1,638	1,707	4,823	582	1,588
Westmeath	15,163	6,341	1,386	1,562	4,034	486	1,354
Wexford	34,664	13,261	3,994	3,411	9,855	1,134	3,009
Wicklow	23,522	9,642	2,416	2,139	6,221	714	2,390
Munster	**237,395**	**95,726**	**21,727**	**27,211**	**63,742**	**7,116**	**21,873**
Clare	24,018	9,863	2,218	2,809	6,194	663	2,271
Cork	77,203	32,403	5,829	8,845	20,911	2,107	7,108
Kerry	39,280	14,412	4,030	5,254	10,845	1,302	3,437
Limerick	40,594	16,734	4,012	4,312	10,318	1,274	3,944
Tipperary NR	16,712	6,596	1,557	1,800	4,686	530	1,543
Tipperary SR	20,298	7,835	2,167	2,146	5,596	722	1,832
Waterford	19,290	7,883	1,914	2,045	5,192	518	1,738
Connacht	**109,567**	**43,140**	**10,260**	**13,249**	**29,006**	**3,630**	**10,282**
Galway	41,730	17,270	4,196	4,365	10,383	1,251	4,265
Leitrim	8,559	3,149	727	1,303	2,369	339	672
Mayo	30,734	11,285	3,088	3,860	8,568	1,114	2,819
Roscommon	13,845	5,477	930	1,882	3,989	457	1,110
Sligo	14,699	5,959	1,319	1,839	3,697	469	1,416
Ulster (part of)	**82,668**	**30,393**	**10,761**	**9,587**	**21,913**	**3,284**	**6,730**
Cavan	16,550	6,474	1,349	2,102	4,786	568	1,271
Donegal	52,316	18,082	8,211	6,026	13,386	2,270	4,341
Monaghan	13,802	5,837	1,201	1,459	3,741	446	1,118

1 See Appendix 2 note on correct number of households.
2 Source : Census of Population.
3 Includes persons looking for first regular job.

Table 29 Persons (aged 15 and over) in other rural households[1] classified by occupation[2]

Province and County	Total	In labour force							Not in labour force
		Agriculture, forestry and fishermen	Producers, makers and repairers	Labourers and unskilled workers (n.e.s.)	Transport and communication workers	Commerce, insurance and finance workers	Professional and technical workers	Others	
State	**687,245**	**27,404**	**88,228**	**30,369**	**22,638**	**43,164**	**42,351**	**90,164**	**342,927**
Leinster	**257,615**	**11,218**	**34,841**	**10,934**	**8,871**	**16,090**	**14,731**	**35,626**	**125,304**
Carlow	10,798	500	1,727	512	403	569	501	1,254	5,332
Dublin	16,290	783	1,579	430	639	1,116	1,194	3,292	7,257
Kildare	29,164	1,399	4,020	1,277	1,040	1,672	1,564	4,503	13,689
Kilkenny	26,539	1,003	3,932	1,177	1,020	1,618	1,498	3,410	12,881
Laoighis	17,130	668	2,376	598	603	1,106	945	2,235	8,599
Longford	10,026	418	1,308	418	260	583	465	1,168	5,406
Louth	18,793	733	2,917	663	754	1,237	1,169	2,397	8,923
Meath	38,320	1,672	4,897	1,588	1,287	2,502	2,456	5,710	18,208
Offaly	17,206	537	2,984	858	515	947	722	1,943	8,700
Westmeath	15,163	504	2,171	632	444	998	958	2,020	7,436
Wexford	34,664	1,966	4,292	1,682	1,187	2,142	1,642	4,344	17,409
Wicklow	23,522	1,035	2,638	1,099	719	1,600	1,617	3,350	11,464
Munster	**237,395**	**9,600**	**29,136**	**10,981**	**7,977**	**14,996**	**14,974**	**29,789**	**119,942**
Clare	24,018	664	2,878	1,102	707	1,504	1,801	3,425	11,937
Cork	77,203	3,410	9,689	3,115	2,677	4,715	5,314	9,312	38,971
Kerry	39,280	1,317	4,613	1,940	1,035	2,571	2,343	4,623	20,838
Limerick	40,594	1,175	5,157	1,900	1,596	2,705	2,571	5,642	19,848
Tipperary NR	16,712	662	2,097	683	685	1,107	886	2,033	8,559
Tipperary SR	20,298	1,212	2,409	915	601	1,334	1,033	2,498	10,296
Waterford	19,290	1,160	2,293	1,326	676	1,060	1,026	2,256	9,493
Connacht	**109,567**	**3,442**	**12,611**	**4,253**	**3,066**	**7,447**	**8,292**	**14,289**	**56,167**
Galway	41,730	1,398	4,802	1,899	1,195	2,942	3,363	5,867	20,264
Leitrim	8,559	317	890	321	208	543	491	1,106	4,683
Mayo	30,734	1,075	3,560	1,126	838	2,070	2,216	3,488	16,361
Roscommon	13,845	354	1,745	398	379	842	932	1,757	7,438
Sligo	14,699	298	1,614	509	446	1,050	1,290	2,071	7,421
Ulster (part of)	**82,668**	**3,144**	**11,640**	**4,201**	**2,724**	**4,631**	**4,354**	**10,460**	**41,514**
Cavan	16,550	586	2,020	677	557	1,044	889	2,050	8,727
Donegal	52,316	2,109	7,443	3,007	1,561	2,840	2,601	6,732	26,023
Monaghan	13,802	449	2,177	517	606	747	864	1,678	6,764

1 See Appendix 2 note on correct number of households.
2 Source : Census of Population.

Table 30 Persons (aged 15 and over) in other rural households[1] classified by marital status[2]

Province and County	Marital status				
	Total	Single	Married	Separated[3]	Widowed
State	**687,245**	**228,100**	**389,524**	**11,494**	**58,127**
Leinster	**257,615**	**87,034**	**146,927**	**4,632**	**19,022**
Carlow	10,798	3,731	6,019	201	847
Dublin	16,290	5,943	9,095	307	945
Kildare	29,164	10,054	16,717	556	1,837
Kilkenny	26,539	8,892	15,139	452	2,056
Laoighis	17,130	5,749	9,712	296	1,373
Longford	10,026	3,304	5,549	156	1,017
Louth	18,793	6,548	10,594	304	1,347
Meath	38,320	12,655	22,494	572	2,599
Offaly	17,206	5,716	9,920	228	1,342
Westmeath	15,163	4,953	8,660	214	1,336
Wexford	34,664	11,629	19,609	699	2,727
Wicklow	23,522	7,860	13,419	647	1,596
Munster	**237,395**	**79,146**	**133,652**	**4,014**	**20,583**
Clare	24,018	7,682	13,764	456	2,116
Cork	77,203	25,898	43,513	1,271	6,521
Kerry	39,280	12,883	21,978	611	3,808
Limerick	40,594	13,651	22,930	630	3,383
Tipperary NR	16,712	5,510	9,447	281	1,474
Tipperary SR	20,298	6,898	11,327	376	1,697
Waterford	19,290	6,624	10,693	389	1,584
Connacht	**109,567**	**33,611**	**63,282**	**1,621**	**11,053**
Galway	41,730	13,144	24,416	603	3,567
Leitrim	8,559	2,678	4,657	146	1,078
Mayo	30,734	9,205	17,800	448	3,281
Roscommon	13,845	3,993	8,001	201	1,650
Sligo	14,699	4,591	8,408	223	1,477
Ulster (part of)	**82,668**	**28,309**	**45,663**	**1,227**	**7,469**
Cavan	16,550	5,309	9,242	199	1,800
Donegal	52,316	18,681	28,346	822	4,467
Monaghan	13,802	4,319	8,075	206	1,202

1 See Appendix 2 note on correct number of households.
2 Source : Census of Population.
3 Including divorced.

Table 31 Persons (aged 15 and over) in urban households[1] classified by principal economic status[2]

Province and County	Principal economic status						
	Total	At work	Unemployed[3]	Retired	Home duties	Unable to work (sick or disabled)	Other
State	**1,423,318**	**643,608**	**145,968**	**115,402**	**313,418**	**37,130**	**167,792**
Leinster	**968,771**	**447,899**	**100,089**	**78,286**	**209,291**	**23,734**	**109,472**
Carlow	12,573	5,289	1,363	978	2,933	411	1,599
Dublin	727,531	341,436	74,884	60,272	151,400	16,918	82,621
Kildare	46,803	23,479	3,526	2,326	10,519	919	6,034
Kilkenny	12,793	5,799	1,170	1,002	3,207	345	1,270
Laoighis	9,174	3,868	1,033	697	2,435	243	898
Longford	4,281	1,750	448	317	1,213	140	413
Louth	40,326	16,350	5,414	3,672	9,277	1,462	4,151
Meath	21,317	9,817	2,188	1,372	5,256	512	2,172
Offaly	14,055	5,621	1,653	1,208	3,579	514	1,480
Westmeath	18,591	8,296	1,560	1,449	4,349	473	2,464
Wexford	22,920	9,277	2,984	1,967	5,896	792	2,004
Wicklow	38,407	16,917	3,866	3,026	9,227	1,005	4,366
Munster	**343,285**	**146,269**	**35,492**	**27,724**	**80,918**	**10,464**	**42,418**
Clare	20,815	10,060	1,850	1,406	4,503	487	2,509
Cork	172,219	73,263	16,548	14,004	41,119	5,294	21,991
Kerry	22,751	9,421	2,298	2,012	5,656	688	2,676
Limerick	55,976	23,416	6,480	4,251	12,054	1,965	7,810
Tipperary NR	13,149	5,445	1,459	1,183	3,337	386	1,339
Tipperary SR	20,276	8,229	2,578	1,820	5,165	676	1,808
Waterford	38,099	16,435	4,279	3,048	9,084	968	4,285
Connacht	**79,092**	**35,358**	**7,152**	**6,591**	**15,791**	**1,779**	**12,421**
Galway	46,563	20,670	4,032	3,503	8,786	949	8,623
Leitrim	959	414	95	103	228	25	94
Mayo	13,852	6,096	1,423	1,328	3,149	339	1,517
Roscommon	5,563	2,501	409	624	1,302	165	562
Sligo	12,155	5,677	1,193	1,033	2,326	301	1,625
Ulster (part of)	**32,170**	**14,082**	**3,235**	**2,801**	**7,418**	**1,153**	**3,481**
Cavan	5,259	2,264	549	433	1,322	187	504
Donegal	17,283	7,824	1,699	1,510	3,627	568	2,055
Monaghan	9,628	3,994	987	858	2,469	398	922

1 See Appendix 2 note on correct number of households.
2 Source : Census of Population.
3 Includes persons looking for first regular job.

Table 32 Persons (aged 15 and over) in urban households[1] classified by occupation[2]

Province and County	Total	In labour force							Not in labour force
		Agriculture, forestry and fishermen	Producers, makers and repairers	Labourers and unskilled workers (n.e.s.)	Transport and communication workers	Commerce, insurance and finance workers	Professional and technical workers	Others	
State	**1,423,318**	**8,723**	**157,512**	**44,637**	**55,668**	**103,982**	**124,249**	**294,805**	**633,742**
Leinster	**968,771**	**5,394**	**103,739**	**28,072**	**39,915**	**68,683**	**86,614**	**215,571**	**420,783**
Carlow	12,573	135	1,790	518	447	913	894	1,955	5,921
Dublin	727,531	2,862	72,885	19,720	31,749	49,852	67,943	171,309	311,211
Kildare	46,803	692	5,473	1,331	1,463	3,462	4,282	10,302	19,798
Kilkenny	12,793	97	1,412	331	394	1,151	1,201	2,383	5,824
Laoighis	9,174	76	1,180	324	357	732	576	1,656	4,273
Longford	4,281	24	522	144	111	358	344	695	2,083
Louth	40,326	253	6,005	1,706	1,530	2,874	2,529	6,867	18,562
Meath	21,317	338	2,837	782	684	1,679	1,783	3,902	9,312
Offaly	14,055	155	2,141	601	407	1,068	842	2,060	6,781
Westmeath	18,591	94	1,887	456	565	1,512	1,653	3,689	8,735
Wexford	22,920	261	3,236	940	876	2,012	1,387	3,549	10,659
Wicklow	38,407	407	4,371	1,219	1,332	3,070	3,180	7,204	17,624
Munster	**343,285**	**2,351**	**41,959**	**13,480**	**12,378**	**26,135**	**26,751**	**58,707**	**161,524**
Clare	20,815	99	2,882	806	793	1,454	1,658	4,218	8,905
Cork	172,219	1,257	20,154	6,365	6,654	12,683	13,947	28,751	82,408
Kerry	22,751	142	2,640	939	590	2,058	1,641	3,709	11,032
Limerick	55,976	198	6,403	1,861	1,937	4,258	4,675	10,564	26,080
Tipperary NR	13,149	119	1,690	616	466	1,112	850	2,051	6,245
Tipperary SR	20,276	279	2,577	999	563	1,803	1,292	3,294	9,469
Waterford	38,099	257	5,613	1,894	1,375	2,767	2,688	6,120	17,385
Connacht	**79,092**	**582**	**7,670**	**2,022**	**2,346**	**6,757**	**8,272**	**14,861**	**36,582**
Galway	46,563	367	4,165	1,043	1,311	3,754	5,079	8,983	21,861
Leitrim	959	–	95	28	30	110	50	196	450
Mayo	13,852	115	1,437	482	402	1,382	1,383	2,318	6,333
Roscommon	5,563	47	557	122	166	569	505	944	2,653
Sligo	12,155	53	1,416	347	437	942	1,255	2,420	5,285
Ulster (part of)	**32,170**	**396**	**4,144**	**1,063**	**1,029**	**2,407**	**2,612**	**5,666**	**14,853**
Cavan	5,259	47	599	218	172	449	386	942	2,446
Donegal	17,283	239	2,209	554	522	1,289	1,539	3,171	7,760
Monaghan	9,628	110	1,336	291	335	669	687	1,553	4,647

1 See Appendix 2 note on correct number of households.
2 Source : Census of Population.

Table 33 Persons (aged 15 and over) in urban households[1] classified by marital status[2]

Province and County	Total	Marital status				
		Single	Married	Separated[3]	Widowed
State	**1,423,318**	**562,395**	**730,791**	**40,915**	**89,217**
Leinster	**968,771**	**383,911**	**496,608**	**29,412**	**58,840**
Carlow	12,573	4,743	6,735	310	785
Dublin	727,531	298,907	361,846	22,821	43,957
Kildare	46,803	15,834	27,697	1,096	2,176
Kilkenny	12,793	4,437	7,127	412	817
Laoighis	9,174	3,234	5,104	186	650
Longford	4,281	1,553	2,300	135	293
Louth	40,326	14,598	21,701	1,265	2,762
Meath	21,317	6,972	12,529	630	1,186
Offaly	14,055	4,843	7,902	308	1,002
Westmeath	18,591	7,205	9,755	413	1,218
Wexford	22,920	8,289	12,319	566	1,746
Wicklow	38,407	13,296	21,593	1,270	2,248
Munster	**343,285**	**132,243**	**179,210**	**8,892**	**22,940**
Clare	20,815	7,537	11,603	581	1,094
Cork	172,219	66,932	89,634	4,101	11,552
Kerry	22,751	8,754	11,766	575	1,656
Limerick	55,976	22,624	28,115	1,638	3,599
Tipperary NR	13,149	4,831	6,931	305	1,082
Tipperary SR	20,276	7,058	11,107	581	1,530
Waterford	38,099	14,507	20,054	1,111	2,427
Connacht	**79,092**	**33,917**	**38,164**	**1,899**	**5,112**
Galway	46,563	21,375	21,415	1,133	2,640
Leitrim	959	324	508	29	98
Mayo	13,852	5,170	7,277	326	1,079
Roscommon	5,563	1,986	2,999	90	488
Sligo	12,155	5,062	5,965	321	807
Ulster (part of)	**32,170**	**12,324**	**16,809**	**712**	**2,325**
Cavan	5,259	1,896	2,844	126	393
Donegal	17,283	6,820	8,959	348	1,156
Monaghan	9,628	3,608	5,006	238	776

1 See Appendix 2 note on correct number of households.
2 Source : Census of Population.
3 Including divorced.

Table 34 Persons in family farm households classified by age[1] and sex[1]

Province and County	Total	Age					
		Under 15	15 - 34	35 - 44	45 - 54	55 - 64	65+
State	**630,950**	**156,608**	**171,658**	**73,586**	**70,454**	**70,248**	**88,396**
Leinster	**163,091**	**41,244**	**46,616**	**19,124**	**18,582**	**17,608**	**19,918**
Carlow	8,323	2,167	2,316	998	930	925	986
Dublin	5,869	1,269	2,072	674	714	606	534
Kildare	12,048	2,921	3,454	1,547	1,464	1,242	1,421
Kilkenny	17,558	4,589	4,962	1,995	1,925	1,896	2,191
Laoighis	15,167	3,980	4,230	1,711	1,687	1,632	1,926
Longford	11,069	2,884	2,862	1,306	1,137	1,290	1,591
Louth	8,785	2,078	2,674	975	1,000	922	1,137
Meath	21,614	5,457	6,393	2,609	2,426	2,300	2,430
Offaly	15,536	3,903	4,432	1,785	1,706	1,716	1,994
Westmeath	14,792	3,661	4,087	1,689	1,714	1,740	1,902
Wexford	22,133	5,802	6,301	2,596	2,651	2,288	2,496
Wicklow	10,196	2,532	2,833	1,240	1,228	1,052	1,311
Munster	**213,137**	**53,614**	**58,866**	**25,275**	**23,962**	**23,693**	**27,727**
Clare	29,426	7,392	7,602	3,548	3,240	3,319	4,325
Cork	67,308	17,010	19,363	7,909	7,411	7,386	8,228
Kerry	40,308	9,875	10,799	4,734	4,625	4,563	5,711
Limerick	27,872	6,991	7,757	3,454	3,215	3,121	3,334
Tipperary NR	17,184	4,410	4,773	2,075	1,910	1,893	2,124
Tipperary SR	18,677	4,712	5,186	2,085	2,124	2,110	2,460
Waterford	12,362	3,223	3,386	1,469	1,438	1,301	1,545
Connacht	**173,660**	**41,649**	**44,281**	**19,957**	**19,082**	**19,871**	**28,820**
Galway	60,023	14,229	16,015	6,799	6,677	6,637	9,667
Leitrim	14,822	3,643	3,617	1,769	1,706	1,700	2,387
Mayo	52,765	12,688	12,933	6,070	5,721	5,967	9,386
Roscommon	27,085	6,455	6,965	3,014	2,935	3,379	4,337
Sligo	18,965	4,633	4,752	2,305	2,044	2,188	3,043
Ulster (part of)	**81,062**	**20,102**	**21,895**	**9,231**	**8,827**	**9,076**	**11,931**
Cavan	23,874	5,968	6,437	2,757	2,528	2,792	3,391
Donegal	37,304	8,980	9,833	4,083	4,212	4,151	6,044
Monaghan	19,884	5,153	5,624	2,390	2,087	2,133	2,496

1 Source : Census of Population.

38

Table 34 Persons in family farm households classified by age[1] and sex[1] (contd.)

Male

Province and County	Age						
	Total	Under 15	15 - 34	35 - 44	45 - 54	55 - 64	65+
State	**342,678**	**80,329**	**96,556**	**39,025**	**38,034**	**39,685**	**49,049**
Leinster	**87,553**	**20,984**	**26,122**	**9,916**	**9,703**	**9,851**	**10,977**
Carlow	4,484	1,082	1,330	514	497	524	535
Dublin	3,025	640	1,062	342	356	335	290
Kildare	6,351	1,448	1,916	776	768	672	772
Kilkenny	9,518	2,367	2,848	1,054	1,023	1,045	1,180
Laoighis	8,188	2,008	2,428	881	882	931	1,059
Longford	6,055	1,479	1,647	702	629	713	884
Louth	4,755	1,120	1,445	525	509	530	626
Meath	11,492	2,739	3,564	1,341	1,241	1,279	1,328
Offaly	8,485	2,028	2,508	932	900	973	1,143
Westmeath	7,997	1,872	2,267	887	883	978	1,110
Wexford	11,770	2,911	3,561	1,322	1,374	1,280	1,321
Wicklow	5,433	1,288	1,546	640	639	591	730
Munster	**115,702**	**27,476**	**33,394**	**13,442**	**12,875**	**13,304**	**15,211**
Clare	16,122	3,764	4,344	1,867	1,819	1,888	2,438
Cork	36,288	8,697	10,941	4,172	3,924	4,063	4,490
Kerry	22,200	5,021	6,194	2,629	2,557	2,619	3,179
Limerick	15,121	3,687	4,375	1,816	1,714	1,751	1,780
Tipperary NR	9,226	2,258	2,679	1,099	996	1,060	1,135
Tipperary SR	10,010	2,393	2,945	1,092	1,082	1,172	1,325
Waterford	6,735	1,656	1,916	767	783	750	863
Connacht	**94,735**	**21,425**	**24,809**	**10,703**	**10,590**	**11,205**	**16,003**
Galway	32,605	7,243	9,025	3,624	3,701	3,705	5,307
Leitrim	8,277	1,898	2,057	974	979	983	1,386
Mayo	28,647	6,637	7,112	3,267	3,176	3,359	5,096
Roscommon	14,791	3,270	3,910	1,614	1,617	1,869	2,511
Sligo	10,415	2,376	2,705	1,223	1,117	1,290	1,704
Ulster (part of)	**44,688**	**10,444**	**12,230**	**4,964**	**4,867**	**5,326**	**6,857**
Cavan	13,102	3,011	3,648	1,513	1,406	1,649	1,874
Donegal	20,638	4,739	5,429	2,190	2,314	2,425	3,542
Monaghan	10,948	2,693	3,154	1,262	1,147	1,252	1,441

1 Source : Census of Population.

Table 34 Persons in family farm households classified by age[1] and sex[1] (contd.)

Female

| Province and County | Total | Age | | | | | | |
		Under 15	15 - 34	35 - 44	45 - 54	55 - 64	65+
State	**288,272**	**76,279**	**75,102**	**34,562**	**32,419**	**30,562**	**39,347**
Leinster	**75,539**	**20,260**	**20,493**	**9,209**	**8,879**	**7,757**	**8,940**
Carlow	3,839	1,085	986	484	433	401	451
Dublin	2,844	629	1,010	332	358	271	244
Kildare	5,697	1,473	1,537	771	697	570	649
Kilkenny	8,040	2,222	2,113	942	902	850	1,011
Laoighis	6,979	1,972	1,802	831	805	702	867
Longford	5,015	1,404	1,216	604	508	577	707
Louth	4,031	958	1,229	450	490	392	512
Meath	10,122	2,718	2,829	1,268	1,184	1,021	1,102
Offaly	7,052	1,875	1,924	853	805	742	851
Westmeath	6,795	1,789	1,819	802	831	762	792
Wexford	10,364	2,890	2,740	1,273	1,277	1,008	1,175
Wicklow	4,763	1,244	1,287	600	589	462	581
Munster	**97,435**	**26,137**	**25,473**	**11,833**	**11,087**	**10,389**	**12,516**
Clare	13,305	3,628	3,257	1,681	1,421	1,430	1,887
Cork	31,020	8,313	8,422	3,737	3,487	3,323	3,738
Kerry	18,108	4,854	4,605	2,105	2,068	1,944	2,532
Limerick	12,750	3,304	3,383	1,639	1,501	1,371	1,554
Tipperary NR	7,958	2,152	2,094	976	914	833	989
Tipperary SR	8,667	2,319	2,241	993	1,042	938	1,134
Waterford	5,627	1,567	1,470	702	655	551	682
Connacht	**78,924**	**20,224**	**19,472**	**9,254**	**8,492**	**8,665**	**12,817**
Galway	27,418	6,986	6,990	3,174	2,976	2,932	4,361
Leitrim	6,545	1,745	1,559	795	727	717	1,001
Mayo	24,117	6,051	5,821	2,803	2,545	2,608	4,290
Roscommon	12,294	3,186	3,055	1,400	1,318	1,510	1,826
Sligo	8,550	2,257	2,047	1,082	927	898	1,339
Ulster (part of)	**36,374**	**9,658**	**9,664**	**4,266**	**3,961**	**3,751**	**5,074**
Cavan	10,772	2,957	2,789	1,245	1,121	1,143	1,517
Donegal	16,666	4,241	4,405	1,893	1,899	1,726	2,502
Monaghan	8,936	2,460	2,470	1,128	941	881	1,055

1 Source : Census of Population.

Table 35 Family farm households classified by number of persons in household[1]

Province and County	Family farm households	Number of persons in family farm household						Total persons
		1	2	3	4	5 - 6	7 +	
State	**169,893**	**26,129**	**34,383**	**27,104**	**25,283**	**38,517**	**18,478**	**630,950**
Leinster	**42,508**	**5,497**	**8,060**	**6,890**	**6,995**	**10,417**	**4,650**	**163,091**
Carlow	2,121	279	370	368	316	523	265	8,323
Dublin	1,468	154	235	220	270	443	146	5,869
Kildare	3,183	381	632	537	555	775	303	12,048
Kilkenny	4,417	496	803	744	686	1,141	547	17,558
Laoighis	3,918	491	758	610	650	974	436	15,167
Longford	3,097	542	631	461	503	678	282	11,069
Louth	2,268	288	401	388	379	554	257	8,785
Meath	5,593	675	1,041	886	970	1,418	603	21,614
Offaly	4,090	576	798	635	677	930	473	15,536
Westmeath	4,102	682	848	658	610	912	392	14,792
Wexford	5,550	594	975	957	924	1,437	663	22,133
Wicklow	2,701	338	566	425	454	633	284	10,196
Munster	**56,245**	**7,909**	**10,687**	**9,276**	**8,766**	**13,493**	**6,114**	**213,137**
Clare	8,207	1,430	1,681	1,330	1,169	1,813	784	29,426
Cork	17,222	2,213	3,069	2,814	2,698	4,406	2,022	67,308
Kerry	10,849	1,676	2,185	1,777	1,605	2,384	1,223	40,308
Limerick	7,366	961	1,392	1,259	1,201	1,817	737	27,872
Tipperary NR	4,440	550	814	726	763	1,098	488	17,184
Tipperary SR	4,921	657	907	866	816	1,162	513	18,677
Waterford	3,240	422	638	506	514	813	347	12,362
Connacht	**48,920**	**8,832**	**10,940**	**7,590**	**6,470**	**9,925**	**5,162**	**173,660**
Galway	16,213	2,635	3,409	2,575	2,161	3,523	1,909	60,023
Leitrim	4,512	991	1,050	683	595	843	351	14,822
Mayo	14,881	2,711	3,441	2,281	1,913	2,876	1,659	52,765
Roscommon	7,799	1,427	1,805	1,214	1,040	1,575	739	27,085
Sligo	5,515	1,068	1,236	837	763	1,108	503	18,965
Ulster (part of)	**22,220**	**3,891**	**4,696**	**3,348**	**3,052**	**4,681**	**2,552**	**81,062**
Cavan	6,701	1,228	1,382	1,027	947	1,440	678	23,874
Donegal	10,214	1,779	2,291	1,543	1,329	2,040	1,232	37,304
Monaghan	5,305	883	1,023	778	777	1,202	642	19,884

1 Source : Census of Population.

Table 36 Family farm households classified by number of persons in household[1] and farm type[2]

Farm type	Family farm households	Number of persons in family farm household						Total persons
		1	2	3	4	5 - 6	7 +	
Total	**169,893**	**26,129**	**34,383**	**27,104**	**25,283**	**38,517**	**18,478**	**630,950**
Specialist tillage	4,787	499	790	697	862	1,383	556	19,438
Specialist dairying	44,906	3,096	7,150	7,816	7,818	12,623	6,402	190,722
Specialist beef production	69,504	14,688	16,745	10,765	8,981	12,639	5,686	229,359
Specialist sheep	14,406	2,529	2,878	2,113	2,053	3,233	1,600	52,937
Mixed grazing livestock	29,579	4,712	5,769	4,573	4,374	6,717	3,434	110,922
Mixed crops and livestock	4,240	410	694	740	743	1,135	518	17,207
Other	2,472	194	357	400	453	786	283	10,365

1 Source : Census of Population.
2 Source : Census of Agriculture.

Table 37 Family farm households classified by nature of occupancy[1]

Province and County	Total	Nature of occupancy						
		Rented local authority	Other rented	Local authority purchase	Owner occupied - mortgage or loan	Owner occupied - no mortgage or loan	Occupied free of rent	Not stated
State	**169,893**	**2,626**	**1,059**	**3,198**	**28,800**	**127,628**	**2,892**	**3,690**
Leinster	**42,508**	**314**	**361**	**723**	**9,143**	**30,438**	**775**	**754**
Carlow	2,121	10	12	27	382	1,621	50	19
Dublin	1,468	4	27	16	425	926	40	31
Kildare	3,183	13	34	29	835	2,153	62	56
Kilkenny	4,417	38	33	41	913	3,287	65	41
Laoighis	3,918	42	32	70	667	2,988	67	52
Longford	3,097	38	22	73	625	2,227	45	68
Louth	2,268	11	25	52	534	1,576	32	38
Meath	5,593	33	59	145	1,468	3,657	110	121
Offaly	4,090	25	35	88	812	2,988	50	92
Westmeath	4,102	29	27	52	960	2,845	85	103
Wexford	5,550	46	36	100	1,009	4,162	108	89
Wicklow	2,701	27	19	30	511	2,007	61	45
Munster	**56,245**	**666**	**293**	**986**	**9,196**	**42,832**	**972**	**1,301**
Clare	8,207	38	41	71	1,200	6,507	145	205
Cork	17,222	87	85	137	2,759	13,465	278	411
Kerry	10,849	376	33	411	1,362	8,195	199	273
Limerick	7,366	93	32	160	1,348	5,427	123	183
Tipperary NR	4,440	20	32	90	818	3,361	67	52
Tipperary SR	4,921	28	40	73	968	3,578	104	128
Waterford	3,240	22	29	44	741	2,299	56	49
Connacht	**48,920**	**1,128**	**241**	**1,084**	**7,272**	**37,404**	**701**	**1,090**
Galway	16,213	308	69	217	2,244	12,734	233	409
Leitrim	4,512	99	24	102	703	3,380	76	127
Mayo	14,881	486	62	411	2,006	11,443	170	304
Roscommon	7,799	138	47	223	1,385	5,765	127	114
Sligo	5,515	97	40	130	935	4,082	96	135
Ulster (part of)	**22,220**	**518**	**165**	**405**	**3,188**	**16,954**	**444**	**545**
Cavan	6,701	58	39	53	1,131	5,146	98	178
Donegal	10,214	436	92	320	1,022	7,838	258	247
Monaghan	5,305	25	34	32	1,035	3,971	88	121

1 Source : Census of Population.

Table 38 Family farm households classified by year dwelling built[1]

Province and County	Total	Year dwelling built							
		before 1919	1919 - 1940	1941 - 1960	1961 - 1970	1971 - 1980	1981 - 1985	1986 or later	not stated
State	**169,893**	**59,789**	**28,526**	**19,889**	**13,699**	**25,623**	**12,318**	**7,647**	**2,401**
Leinster	**42,508**	**17,125**	**5,272**	**3,987**	**3,635**	**7,081**	**2,921**	**2,031**	**456**
Carlow	2,121	1,093	242	135	128	273	130	104	16
Dublin	1,468	396	160	159	204	311	104	106	27
Kildare	3,183	1,081	377	350	281	641	216	200	36
Kilkenny	4,417	2,157	453	294	265	719	273	217	38
Laoighis	3,918	1,710	482	322	304	628	251	178	42
Longford	3,097	1,241	401	317	268	485	235	122	27
Louth	2,268	890	292	159	236	418	145	101	28
Meath	5,593	1,652	979	732	576	982	382	228	62
Offaly	4,090	1,381	622	497	430	652	301	162	44
Westmeath	4,102	1,565	511	497	392	637	307	171	23
Wexford	5,550	2,667	516	371	383	880	379	290	65
Wicklow	2,701	1,291	238	153	167	455	197	151	48
Munster	**56,245**	**22,696**	**8,653**	**5,358**	**3,978**	**8,411**	**3,823**	**2,555**	**771**
Clare	8,207	3,089	1,345	975	705	1,039	557	364	134
Cork	17,222	8,170	2,524	1,197	947	2,356	1,012	781	234
Kerry	10,849	2,948	2,132	1,613	901	1,704	957	455	138
Limerick	7,366	2,789	1,081	699	564	1,266	492	357	119
Tipperary NR	4,440	1,886	611	344	331	721	293	211	42
Tipperary SR	4,921	2,312	637	356	324	727	289	207	70
Waterford	3,240	1,503	322	174	206	597	222	180	34
Connacht	**48,920**	**11,910**	**11,137**	**8,226**	**4,372**	**6,724**	**3,799**	**2,016**	**737**
Galway	16,213	3,479	3,560	2,924	1,721	2,506	1,187	588	249
Leitrim	4,512	1,672	775	639	265	492	372	199	98
Mayo	14,881	2,687	4,112	2,716	1,262	1,986	1,249	647	222
Roscommon	7,799	2,265	1,579	1,252	686	1,066	587	302	62
Sligo	5,515	1,806	1,110	695	439	674	403	280	106
Ulster (part of)	**22,220**	**8,058**	**3,465**	**2,317**	**1,714**	**3,408**	**1,775**	**1,045**	**437**
Cavan	6,701	2,522	1,025	910	537	820	470	296	122
Donegal	10,214	3,526	1,367	991	898	1,765	948	493	226
Monaghan	5,305	2,010	1,073	416	279	823	358	256	88

1 Source : Census of Population.

Table 39 Family farm households classified by method of heating[1]

Province and County	Total	Open fire only	Open fire, water heating back boiler	Open fire, back boiler central heating	Closed solid fuel room heating only	Closed solid fuel room and water heating	Closed solid fuel central heating	Oil fired central heating	Dual system central heating	Other
State	169,893	21,733	14,509	15,299	14,581	31,633	32,330	25,296	6,255	8,257
Leinster	42,508	4,116	2,631	3,551	3,330	7,560	9,460	8,091	1,868	1,900
Carlow	2,121	241	74	122	260	358	379	491	96	100
Dublin	1,468	182	118	165	35	99	176	513	84	96
Kildare	3,183	236	172	235	147	483	768	817	164	161
Kilkenny	4,417	567	275	366	332	626	808	1,067	198	178
Laoighis	3,918	258	187	241	434	795	1,108	575	177	143
Longford	3,097	307	213	221	373	740	749	228	111	154
Louth	2,268	263	206	287	93	262	376	563	99	119
Meath	5,593	392	351	494	360	859	1,229	1,371	296	242
Offaly	4,090	277	197	276	432	984	1,360	314	113	138
Westmeath	4,102	353	238	277	374	959	1,059	480	186	177
Wexford	5,550	754	457	695	294	883	905	1,086	218	256
Wicklow	2,701	287	143	173	197	512	542	585	126	136
Munster	56,245	9,066	5,753	6,013	3,867	8,375	7,702	10,256	2,149	3,063
Clare	8,207	1,453	869	803	643	1,563	1,262	963	273	377
Cork	17,222	3,208	1,905	2,228	886	1,926	1,770	3,543	686	1,071
Kerry	10,849	1,599	1,092	881	916	2,292	1,823	1,489	259	496
Limerick	7,366	979	687	757	542	1,003	963	1,582	384	469
Tipperary NR	4,440	362	282	277	528	848	1,006	783	177	177
Tipperary SR	4,921	730	473	566	308	549	622	1,130	243	300
Waterford	3,240	736	446	500	43	193	256	766	127	172
Connacht	48,920	6,855	4,753	4,306	4,520	10,842	9,926	4,142	1,546	2,031
Galway	16,213	2,053	1,673	1,271	1,424	3,901	3,053	1,480	559	799
Leitrim	4,512	524	263	241	753	989	939	372	118	313
Mayo	14,881	2,417	1,812	1,797	1,032	2,919	2,877	1,146	486	395
Roscommon	7,799	1,080	663	660	674	1,780	1,836	595	213	298
Sligo	5,515	781	342	338	637	1,253	1,221	549	169	224
Ulster (part of)	22,220	1,697	1,372	1,428	2,864	4,855	5,242	2,807	691	1,264
Cavan	6,701	386	272	312	1,019	1,525	1,691	913	202	380
Donegal	10,214	1,017	889	836	1,164	2,357	2,148	996	307	500
Monaghan	5,305	293	211	280	680	973	1,403	898	182	385

1 Source : Census of Population.

Table 40 Family farm households classified by piped water supply[1]

Province and County	Total	Piped water supply				No piped water	Not stated
		Public mains	Local authority group scheme	Private group scheme	Other private source		
State	**169,893**	**39,168**	**29,005**	**26,391**	**67,531**	**6,135**	**1,664**
Leinster	**42,508**	**9,916**	**4,751**	**3,949**	**22,350**	**1,226**	**316**
Carlow	2,121	298	134	218	1,389	67	14
Dublin	1,468	1,178	35	29	199	9	18
Kildare	3,183	1,080	365	183	1,500	28	27
Kilkenny	4,417	847	377	525	2,551	95	22
Laoighis	3,918	627	446	448	2,223	141	34
Longford	3,097	1,192	447	265	1,019	158	16
Louth	2,268	555	275	267	1,101	51	19
Meath	5,593	757	768	468	3,414	157	29
Offaly	4,090	716	752	694	1,730	166	32
Westmeath	4,102	995	520	212	2,165	193	17
Wexford	5,550	1,251	559	420	3,194	72	54
Wicklow	2,701	419	74	220	1,864	90	35
Munster	**56,245**	**14,847**	**8,906**	**5,616**	**24,551**	**1,769**	**555**
Clare	8,207	1,977	2,239	1,295	2,153	439	104
Cork	17,222	4,181	1,287	1,376	9,751	478	148
Kerry	10,849	3,481	2,009	654	4,230	373	102
Limerick	7,366	1,458	1,415	1,034	3,207	184	67
Tipperary NR	4,440	554	598	706	2,414	126	42
Tipperary SR	4,921	2,509	1,134	221	921	74	62
Waterford	3,240	687	223	330	1,875	95	30
Connacht	**48,920**	**9,257**	**12,115**	**12,173**	**12,718**	**2,180**	**477**
Galway	16,213	2,840	3,253	4,196	5,036	692	196
Leitrim	4,512	804	1,025	1,081	1,206	324	72
Mayo	14,881	1,984	4,164	4,615	3,507	493	118
Roscommon	7,799	2,305	2,295	1,308	1,581	282	28
Sligo	5,515	1,324	1,379	973	1,389	388	63
Ulster (part of)	**22,220**	**5,147**	**3,232**	**4,653**	**7,911**	**960**	**316**
Cavan	6,701	721	859	2,208	2,509	319	85
Donegal	10,214	3,945	1,613	590	3,439	447	181
Monaghan	5,305	481	760	1,855	1,963	194	51

1 Source : Census of Population.

Appendices

Appendix 1

1991 Censuses of Agriculture and Population publications

Census of Agriculture, June 1991 - First Results (Pl. 9418, December 1992)
Census of Agriculture, June 1991 - Detailed Results (Pl. 0740, May 1994)
Census of Agriculture, June 1991 - Rural District Results (Pn 2213, December 1995)

Census 1991, Volume 1 - Population classified by Area (Pl. 9877, June 1993)
Census 1991, Volume 2 - Ages and Marital Status (Pn 0815, June 1994)
Census 1991, Volume 3 - Household Composition & Family Units (Pn 1221, December 1994)
Census 1991, Volume 4 - Principal Economic Status and Industries (Pn 1827, August 1995)
Census 1991, Volume 5 - Religion (Pn 2034, November 1995)
Census 1991, Volume 6 - Occupations (Pn 2102, December 1995)
Census 1991, Volume 7 - An Ghaeilge Irish Language (Pn 2295, February 1996)
Census 1991, Volume 8 - Usual Residence and Migration Birthplaces (Pn 2754, June 1996)
Census 1991, Volume 9 - Education (Pn 3243, December 1996)
Census 1991, Volume 10 - Housing (Pn 3505, February 1997)
Census 1991, Volume 11 - Travel to Work, School and College (Pn 4013, July 1997)

Appendix 2

Methodology

The linkage between both Censuses was primarily achieved though a question (Q.24) on the Census of Population form relating to farming activity. Each person aged 15 years and over was asked to indicate if they were engaged in farming on their own-account.

FARMING ACTIVITY

Is the person engaged at all in farming on own-account
(on land owned or rented by the person)?
If so, answer "Yes" if the area farmed is 1 acre or more,
distinguishing whether farming is a principal or subsidiary activity.
Otherwise, answer "No".

(See Notes)

Q.24

Yes – principal activity.............. ☐
Yes - part-time/subsidiary activity ☐
No .... ☐

At the end of the 1991 Census of Population fieldwork, particulars relating to each person recorded as being engaged in farming on own-account were taken from summary Census of Population lists and entered onto Census of Agriculture questionnaires.

The details transferred were the person's name, address, schedule and line number as well as the County, Enumeration Area and District Electoral Division relating to where the person was enumerated. These details enabled the linkage to be made between the family farm operator in the Census of Agriculture and the farmer's household in the Census of Population. The line number allowed the family farm operator to be individually identified in the Census of Population return.

The identification of farms as part of the Census of Agriculture fieldwork also involved the systematic use of the following sources:

- lists of names of landowners extracted from the 1980 Census of Agriculture records (updated where subsequent sample surveys had been conducted);

- lists provided by the Department of Agriculture and Food from its administrative registers;

- information obtained during the fieldwork coupled with the enumerator's local knowledge.

These names were cross-checked against the full list of heads of household names compiled from the Census of Population. If a match was found for households where a match had not already been obtained through the filter question, then the required Census of Population identification details were entered onto a Census of Agriculture questionnaire. The interviewers then called to these households to establish whether they were engaged in farming.

A total of 170,578 farms were recorded in the Census of Agriculture. Of these, 169,893 were family farms. The linkage procedures matched 154,953 family farms and Census of Population households but for some of these family farms, the match had not been made down to the individual family farm operator. Accordingly, these were treated as unmatched in the grossing process. Over 81 per cent of family farms (138,270) were matched at an individual level (the farm operator) with the Census of Population file.

The 81 per cent were composed of 75 per cent from the filter question contained in the Census of Population. The 1980 Census of Agriculture contributed a further 3 per cent. A further 2 per cent were identified from the lists provided by the Department of Agriculture and Food. Less than 1 per cent were identified by the enumerator during the fieldwork and subsequently fully linked to the COP file.

In many cases the family farm operator would have appeared in all three listings. Hence the 2 per cent credited to the Department of Agriculture and Food would have been considerably larger had it been the primary source for the identification of farms. However, an examination of family farms that were only matched with a COP household and not at an individual level, showed that a higher proportion of partial matches occurred in the indirect sources (1980 Census and Department of Agriculture listings).

After the completion of the fieldwork, CSO staff examined all completed Census of Agriculture questionnaires where a schedule match had not been found with the Census of Population. This work was done by examining the heads of households recorded in the same townland during the Census of Population. If a match was found (based on the full-name and response to the Census of Population filter question), the farmer's Census of Population reference number was added to the Census of Agriculture file. This examination resulted in a linkage being found for a further 5,700 farms.

Census of Agriculture farms which were linked to a Census of Population household were grossed to the 169,893 family farms recorded in the Census of Agriculture using county and farm size classes as grossing strata. Because it was necessary to gross for unmatched Census of Agriculture family farms, the total number of private households in this publication exceeds the number of households actually returned in the Census of Population. These extra households represented the difference between the matched number of family farm households and the number recorded in the Census of Agriculture. The unmatched family farms would have been predominantly classified in the detailed tables as other rural households. Hence a significant number of the members of other rural households were classified as belonging to the broad occupation group *Agriculture*.

As the methodology was new and quite complex, an evaluation of the accuracy of the linkages between a farm in the Census of Agriculture and the corresponding farm household in the Census of Population was undertaken. A sample of 14 per cent distributed across all counties was selected for checking. The Census of Agriculture holder's name was compared with the name of the head of household in the Census of Population. There was a full match for 81 per cent with a further 14 per cent matching on surname only. The latter would mainly have related to cases where the holder or family farm operator was not recorded as the head of household in the Census of Population. The 5 per cent of family farms that were not matched, even at surname level, were partially due to the family farm operator being absent on Census night.

Appendix 3

Glossary

Census of Agriculture

Census of Agriculture: A Census of Agriculture was conducted in June 1991 in accordance with the Statistics (Census of Agriculture) Order, 1991 (S.I. no. 126 of 1991). It was conducted by interview using the field force from the April 1991 Census of Population. The objective was to identify all operational farms in the country and to obtain details on the agricultural activities undertaken on them.

Farm: All farms where the agricultural area used was at least 1 hectare (2.4711 acres) were covered in the Census as well as farms with less than 1 hectare involved in intensive production (e.g. pigs and poultry). A farm was defined as:

> *a single unit, both technically and economically, which has a single management and which produces agricultural products*

This definition was adopted by all European Union countries for the EU surveys on the structure of agricultural holdings.

Area farmed: The area farmed was defined as the combined area under crops, silage, hay, pasture and rough grazing land in use (including fallow and set-aside land). Areas taken up by roads, tracks, water, bog, marsh, rocks, unused rough grazing land, buildings etc. were excluded. Commonage used by the farm was not included as part of the area farmed but livestock etc. held on such land were returned as belonging to the farm. The area farmed could consist entirely of owned or rented land or a combination of both. In the case of intensive units, it could consist entirely of buildings.

Family farms: Family farms were broadly defined as farms which were operated as family based enterprises (including the small number which were registered as commercial concerns). Thus only those farms registered as companies which paid all their workers as employees (including management), as well as farms connected with institutions (e.g. schools, colleges, religious communities, prisons, etc.), were classified as non-family farms. Less than 700 farms fell into this category. For purposes of analysis the holder of a family farm was included as part of the Census of Agriculture farm labour force irrespective of whether he/she contributed to the labour input of the farm. Non-family farms were mainly involved in specialist pig and poultry rearing.

Family farm operator: A family farm operator was identified in each Census of Agriculture family farm. He/she was described as the holder in the Census of Agriculture. The owner and the family farm operator was usually the same person. Where the farm was in joint ownership, the person designated as holder was determined by the Census interviewee.

Location: The classification of farms by county was based on the location of the farm residence. This generally coincided with the location of the farm headquarters or farmyard but in a small number of cases, it resulted in farms that were located in one county being classified to another county.

Farm type: An EU-wide system known as the *Community Farm Typology* was developed for the purposes of classifying farms into homogeneous groups based on the type of farming activity engaged in. A feature of this classification is the distinction between *specialist* and *mixed* farms. Specialist farms were those where a particular activity such as tillage or dairying accounted for at least two-thirds of the farm's total economic size.

Farm workforce: Details in respect of all persons aged 15 years and over who contributed to farmwork in the twelve months preceding the Census were separately recorded in the Census of Agriculture. Persons in the farm workforce need not have been members of the family farm household. This publication concerns members of the family farm household and their number and details have been taken from the Census of Population questionnaire without reference to whether they were part of the farm workforce.

Only one member of the farm workforce, the family farm operator, was identified during the linkage of both census files. No attempt was made to identify the individual Census of Population record for any other member of the farm workforce. It can be assumed that most other family members of the farm workforce were recorded as members of the family farm household on Census night. However, some of them may have been normally resident in a different household or may have been temporarily absent on Census night.

Census of Population

Census of Population: A Census of Population was taken on the night of Sunday, 21 April 1991 in accordance with the Statistics (Census of Population) Order 1991 (S.I. no. 62 of 1991).

Head of household: A head of household was identified in every household. He/she was used as the focal point for comparisons between family farm, other rural and urban households. Any adult member of a private household, present on Census night, could be returned as the head according as the household members considered appropriate. Any one person, or group of persons with common housekeeping arrangements, separately occupying all or part of a private house, flats, apartment or other private habitation of any kind was regarded as a private household for Census purposes. Non-private households (institutions etc.) have been excluded from this publication.

Household type: Three types of households were identified for the purposes of this publication – family farm, other rural and urban. Family farm households are those households which were recorded as involved in farming on their own-account in the 1991 Census of Agriculture. Around 2 per cent of family farms were located in urban areas. Urban households were regarded as households located in population clusters of 1,500 or more inhabitants excluding the 2 per cent of households that were classified as family farm households. Other rural households comprised all other households. For presentation purposes, urban households rather than the more strictly correct other urban households has been used throughout this publication.

Household members: The census figures relate to the *de facto* population. Visitors present on census night as well as those in residence were recorded as household members. Usual residents temporarily absent from the household were excluded. This definition impacts to a minor extent on household size.

Marital status: This information was collected on the basis of the *de facto* rather than the legal status.

Principal economic status: This question was asked of all persons aged 15 years and over. The labour force comprises persons whose principal economic status was at work, seeking regular work for the first time or unemployed having lost or given up their previous job. Persons outside of the labour force include those engaged on home duties, students and retired persons.

Occupation: All persons aged 15 years and over who were at work, unemployed or retired were classified in the Census of Population according to their usual (or previous) principal occupation. Nearly one-third of family farm operators had a principal occupation outside of farming.

Labour force: Only those at work, seeking regular work for the first time or unemployed are in the labour force. Family farm operators who gave their principal economic status as retired are classified as *not in the labour force* in the detailed occupation tables (e.g. Table 15). Hence they are not classified to *Agriculture* even if their previous occupation was farmer.

COP farmer: This category is derived from the occupation code. Retired farmers are included. Agricultural related jobs such as farm labourers are not included.

Religion: Persons were asked to state their particular religious denomination. Persons who did not answer this question were included in the category *other*.

Education: This question was asked of persons whose education had ceased. It related to the highest level of education (full-time or part-time) which was actually completed.